First World War
and Army of Occupation
War Diary
France, Belgium and Germany

38 DIVISION
115 Infantry Brigade,
Brigade Machine Gun Company
2 March 1916 - 28 February 1918

WO95/2562/3

The Naval & Military Press Ltd
www.nmarchive.com
Published in association with The National Archives

Published by

The Naval & Military Press Ltd

Unit 10 Ridgewood Industrial Park,

Uckfield, East Sussex,

TN22 5QE England

Tel: +44 (0) 1825 749494

www.naval-military-press.com

www.nmarchive.com

This diary has been reprinted in facsimile from the original. Any imperfections are inevitably reproduced and the quality may fall short of modern type and cartographic standards.

© **Crown Copyright**
Images reproduced by permission of The National Archives, London, England, 2015.

Contents

Document type	Place/Title	Date From	Date To
Heading	WO95/2562/3 38 Divn IIs Inf Brig Brigade M/G Co 1916 March 1918 Feb		
Heading	38th Division 115th Infy Bde 115th Machine Gun Coy Mar 1916-Feb 1918		
Heading	War Diary Of 115 Machine Gun Company Machine Gun Corps From 2nd March 1916 To 31st May 1916		
Miscellaneous	Roll Of Officers		
War Diary	Belton Pk Grantham	02/03/1916	31/03/1916
War Diary	Belton Pk Grantham	22/03/1916	31/03/1916
Heading	War Diary 115 Machine Gun Company From 1st April 1916 To 30th April 1916		
War Diary	Belton Pk Grantham	01/04/1916	28/04/1916
War Diary	Belton Pk Grantham	11/04/1916	30/04/1916
War Diary	Belton Pk Grantham	16/04/1916	30/04/1916
War Diary	Belton Pk Grantham	01/05/1916	15/05/1916
Heading	War Diary Of 115 Machine Gun Company From 1st May 1916 To 31st May 1916		
War Diary	Belton Park Grantham	16/05/1916	17/05/1916
War Diary	Havre	18/05/1916	19/05/1916
War Diary	BEF	19/05/1916	19/05/1916
War Diary	Le Drumez	20/05/1916	26/05/1916
War Diary	Les Puresbecques	27/05/1916	31/05/1916
Heading	War Diary 115 Machine Gun Company From 1st June 1916 To 20th June 1916		
War Diary	Les Puresbecqes	01/06/1916	05/06/1916
Miscellaneous	Situation Of Machine Guns In Fauquissart Sector		
War Diary	Laventie	12/06/1916	12/06/1916
War Diary	Robecq	13/06/1916	14/06/1916
War Diary	Auchel	15/06/1916	15/06/1916
War Diary	Herlin-Le-Vert	16/06/1916	21/06/1916
War Diary	Laventie	05/06/1916	11/06/1916
War Diary	Herlin-Le-Vert	22/06/1916	26/06/1916
War Diary	Beauvoir	27/06/1916	27/06/1916
War Diary	Longuevillette	28/06/1916	01/07/1916
Heading	115th Inf. Bde. 38th Div. 115th Machine Gun Company July 1916		
Heading	War Diary Of 115 M.G. Coy From 1st July 1916 To 31st July 1916		
War Diary	Toutencourt	01/07/1916	01/07/1916
War Diary	Acheux	02/07/1916	04/07/1916
War Diary	Buire-Sur-Ancre	05/07/1916	05/07/1916
War Diary	Mametz	06/07/1916	13/07/1916
War Diary	Warloy Baillon	13/07/1916	13/07/1916
War Diary	Couin	14/07/1916	14/07/1916
War Diary	Courcelles Au-Bois	14/07/1916	28/07/1916
War Diary	Bus-Les-Artois	29/07/1916	30/07/1916
War Diary	Wulverdinghe	31/07/1916	31/07/1916
Heading	War Diary 115 Machine Gun Company From 1/8/16-1/9/16		
War Diary	Wulverdinghe	01/08/1916	02/08/1916

War Diary	Bollezeele	03/08/1916	19/08/1916
War Diary	Sheet 28 N.W. A.23.c.5.8	19/08/1916	20/08/1916
War Diary	Cy. H. QS C.25.a.7.3	21/08/1916	21/08/1916
War Diary	Canal Bank C.25.a.7.3 (Sheet 28. N.W)	21/08/1916	25/08/1916
War Diary	Canal Bank C.25.a.7.3	25/08/1916	31/08/1916
Heading	115th Machine Gun Company From 1st To 30th September		
War Diary	Canal Bank C25.a7.3	01/09/1916	05/09/1916
War Diary	Canal Bank C.19.c.3.6	05/09/1916	18/09/1916
War Diary	S Camp A 22.d 8.3	19/09/1916	30/09/1916
War Diary	Canal Bank C 25a.7.3	03/09/1916	06/09/1916
War Diary	Canal Bank C.19.c.3.6	07/09/1916	18/09/1916
War Diary	S Camp A.22d.8.3	19/09/1916	23/09/1916
War Diary	Camp "S"	24/09/1916	30/09/1916
Heading	115 Machine Gun Coy From 1st To 31st October 1916		
War Diary	Camp "S" A22.d. 8.3	01/10/1916	03/10/1916
War Diary	Canal Bank	03/10/1916	12/10/1916
War Diary	Canal Bk	13/10/1916	18/10/1916
War Diary	Canal Bank	19/10/1916	22/10/1916
War Diary	Canal Bk	23/10/1916	23/10/1916
War Diary	Canal Bank	24/10/1916	25/10/1916
War Diary	Canal Bk	25/10/1916	25/10/1916
War Diary	Camp S a22. d. 8.5	26/10/1916	27/10/1916
War Diary	Camp "S"	27/10/1916	31/10/1916
Heading	115 M.G. Coy November 1st To 30th 1916 Vol 7		
War Diary	'S' Camp	01/11/1916	04/11/1916
War Diary	M.G. Farm H.5.c. 9.9	04/11/1916	04/11/1916
War Diary	M.G. Farm	04/11/1916	14/11/1916
War Diary	Burgomaster Farm	15/11/1916	16/11/1916
War Diary	Canal Bank	17/11/1916	17/11/1916
War Diary	Canal Bk	17/11/1916	23/11/1916
War Diary	Canal Bank	24/11/1916	25/11/1916
War Diary	Camp "S"	25/11/1916	30/11/1916
Heading	115 Machine Gun Company December 1st To December 31st 1916		
War Diary	'S" Camp A 23 G 48	01/12/1918	04/12/1918
War Diary	Canal Bk G9 C 2.6	04/12/1916	11/12/1916
War Diary	'S' Camp	12/12/1916	12/12/1916
War Diary	Decouck Fm B. 13 B.2.8	12/12/1916	13/12/1916
War Diary	Decouck Fm	14/12/1916	18/12/1916
War Diary	Decouck Farm	19/12/1916	23/12/1916
War Diary	Decouck Fm	23/12/1916	30/12/1916
War Diary	Bollezeele	31/12/1916	31/12/1916
Heading	155 M.G. Co. Jan 1st to Jan 31st 1917		
War Diary	Bollezeele	01/01/1917	13/01/1917
War Diary	'E' Camp	14/01/1917	15/01/1917
War Diary	'S' Camp Tranches	16/01/1917	19/01/1917
War Diary	Trenches	19/01/1917	31/01/1917
Heading	From 1st February 1917 To 28th February 1917 Vol 10		
War Diary	Decouck Farm	01/02/1917	08/02/1917
War Diary	Emile Farm	08/01/1917	28/02/1917
Heading	115th Machine Gun Company March 1st To March 31st 1917 Vol XI		
War Diary	Emile Farm	01/03/1917	10/03/1917
War Diary	Mouton Farm	11/03/1917	25/04/1917
War Diary	Mouton Fm	25/04/1917	30/04/1917

Heading	115 Machine Gun Company May 1st To May 31st 1917 Vol 13		
War Diary	Mouton Fm	01/05/1917	02/05/1917
War Diary	Millain	03/05/1917	16/05/1917
War Diary	Herzeele	17/05/1917	21/05/1917
War Diary	Mouton Farm	21/05/1917	31/05/1917
Heading	115 Machine Gun Company 1st June To 30th June 1917		
War Diary	Mouton Farm	01/06/1917	14/06/1917
War Diary	Vox Vrie A 10c 8.2	18/06/1917	27/06/1917
War Diary	Caestre	27/06/1917	28/06/1917
War Diary	Febvin-Palfart	28/06/1917	30/06/1917
Heading	115th Company Machine Gun Corps. War Diary 1st To 31st July 1917		
War Diary	Febvin-Palfart	01/07/1917	16/07/1917
War Diary	Houleron	16/07/1917	17/07/1917
War Diary	L'Egerreest	17/07/1917	18/07/1917
War Diary	Le Garreux	18/07/1917	19/07/1917
War Diary	Proven	19/07/1917	21/07/1917
War Diary	St. Sixte	21/07/1917	27/07/1917
War Diary	Ypres Salient	27/07/1917	31/07/1917
Heading	War Diary 115 Machine Gun Company August 1917 Vol 16		
War Diary	Ypres Salient	01/08/1917	06/08/1917
War Diary	St. Sixte	06/07/1917	18/08/1917
War Diary	Langemarck	18/08/1917	30/08/1917
War Diary	L.2. Elverdinghe	30/08/1917	31/08/1917
Heading	115 Machine Gun Company 1st September To 30th September 1917 Vol 17		
War Diary	Malakoff Farm	01/09/1917	05/09/1917
War Diary	On The R Steenbeek	05/09/1917	10/09/1917
War Diary	P5 Area	11/09/1917	12/09/1917
War Diary	Morbecque	13/09/1917	13/09/1917
War Diary	Estaires	14/09/1917	14/09/1917
War Diary	La Gorgue	15/09/1917	16/09/1917
War Diary	Armentieres	17/09/1917	30/09/1917
Heading	115 Machine Gun Company War Diary October 1917 Vol 18		
War Diary	Armentieres	01/10/1917	21/10/1917
War Diary	Armentieres	20/10/1917	31/10/1917
Heading	115 Machine Gun Company War Diary November 1917 Vol 19		
War Diary	Armentieres	01/11/1917	10/11/1917
Miscellaneous	To DMGO 38th Division	08/11/1917	08/11/1917
War Diary	Armentieres	11/11/1917	30/11/1917
Heading	115 Machine Gun Coy. War Diary. December 1917 Vol 20		
War Diary	Armentieres	01/12/1917	19/12/1917
War Diary	Estaires	20/12/1917	05/01/1918
War Diary	Doulieu	06/01/1918	12/01/1918
War Diary	Estaires	13/01/1918	15/01/1918
War Diary	Garbecques	16/01/1918	16/01/1918
War Diary	Enguinegatte	17/01/1918	30/01/1918
War Diary	Garbecques	31/01/1918	31/01/1918
Heading	115 Machine Gun Company War Diary February 1918 Vol 22		

War Diary	Estaires	01/02/1918	13/02/1918
War Diary	Wez Macquart Sector 47A	14/02/1918	28/02/1918
Heading	WO95/2562/4 38 Divn 115 Inf Brig Trench Mortar Bty 1916 July & Aug		

WO 95 2-562/3

36 DIVN
115 INF. BRIG

BRIGADE M/G CO
MARCH
1916 ~~JULY~~ - 1918 FEB

38TH DIVISION
115TH INFY BDE

115TH MACHINE GUN COY
MAR 1916-FEB 1918

38TH DIVISION
115TH INFY BDE

Army Form C. 2118.

WAR DIARY
or
INTELLIGENCE SUMMARY
(Erase heading not required.)

115 M.G.C.

XXXVIII

For March — May 1.1.

Confidential.
War Diary
of
115 Machine Gun Company,
Machine Gun Corps.

From 2nd March 1916
(date of formation)
To 31st May March 1916.

Place	Date	Hour	Summary of Events and Information	Remarks and references to Appendices

2449 Wt. W14957/M90 750,000 1/16 J.B.C. & A. Forms/C.2118/12.

Army Form C. 2118.

WAR DIARY
or
INTELLIGENCE SUMMARY
(Erase heading not required.)

Place	Date	Hour	Summary of Events and Information	Remarks and references to Appendices

ROLL OF OFFICERS

COMMANDING OFFICER:-

CAPTAIN ERNEST DALZEL JOB   28th LONDON (ARTISTS) RIFLES

SECOND IN COMMAND:-

2nd Lieut. CHARLES HOWARD JOHNSON   16th THE KING'S L'POOL REGT.

SECTION OFFICERS:-

2nd LIEUT. JOHN FRANK ALLIN   9th ROYAL BERKS. REGT.
2nd LIEUT. ALFRED DAVIS   15th THE KING'S L'POOL REGT.
2nd LIEUT. LINCOLN WYCHERLEY EVANS   6th KING'S SHROPSHIRE L.I.
2nd LIEUT. ALEXANDER GIRVAN   9th ROYAL SCOTS. Fus.
2nd LIEUT. GEOFFREY THOMAS HALE   7th ROYAL BERKS REGT.
2nd LIEUT. ARTHUR MAURICE SOUTHON   9th GLOUCESTER. REGT.
2nd LIEUT. ERNEST YEARDLEY   15th YORK & LANC. REGT.

TRANSPORT OFFICER:-

2nd LIEUT. GEORGE LONDON   3/2 County of LONDON Yeo.

Army Form C. 2118.

WAR DIARY
or
INTELLIGENCE SUMMARY
(Erase heading not required.)

Instructions regarding War Diaries and Intelligence Summaries are contained in F. S. Regs., Part II. and the Staff Manual respectively. Title Pages will be prepared in manuscript.

Place	Date	Hour	Summary of Events and Information	Remarks and references to Appendices
Belton Pk Grantham	2/3/16		Company formed under Lieut. C.V. Walker 11th K.O.Y.L.I. and 2.Lt J.Fielder (9th R. Berks)	
	3/3/16		1 Sergt and 5 men reported.	
			1 Sergt and 28 men reported.	
			The following huts taken over for the Company in B. Lines. A 4. (5) for Coy Store room + orderly Room. A.5, 76, B4, 5+6 for men	
	4/3/16		1 Sgt + 33 men went on 6 days final leave	
	6/3/16		2nd Lt. To.B. ERNEST DALZEL. 28th LONDON (ARTISTS RIFLES) took over command of Company.	
	7/3/16		2nd Lt! YEARDLEY ERNEST. 15th YORKS + 2 NCOS reported.	
	8/3/16		Lt. WALKER. C.V. transferred from Company.	
	9.3.16	MN	34 NCO's + men returned from final leave.	
	10.3.16		7 men reported. Training of the gunners commenced.	
	11.3.16		18 men reported (new arrivals)	
	13.3.16		58 men reported.	
	14.3.16		45 NCO's + men went on final leave.	
	16.3.16		37 NCO's went on final leave.	
	19.3.16	MN	42 NCO's returned from final leave.	
	20.3.16	MN	3 men returned from final leave (new arrivals + men reported)	
	21.3.16		37 NCO's + men returned from final leave	
	10/31/16		During this period the elementary training & programmes was carried on by the available officers of the Company under the supervision of the staff of the Training Centre.	

Army Form C. 2118.

WAR DIARY
or
INTELLIGENCE SUMMARY
(Erase heading not required.)

Place	Date	Hour	Summary of Events and Information	Remarks and references to Appendices
Belton Pk Grantham	28/3/16		The following officers posted to the Company, reported for duty. 2nd Lt. EVANS. L.W. 6th K.S.L.I. " DAVIS. A. 15th KINGS (L.P.) REGT. " SOUTHON. A.M. 11th GLOUCESTERS. " HALE. G.T. 7th ROYAL BERKS. " LEWIS. D.A. 2/1st WELSH.	
	29/3/16		Company divided into 4 sections and officers posted as follows. No 1 Section. 2nd Lts. YEARDLEY. E. and LEWIS. D.A. 2 " " SOUTHON. A.M. " DAVIS. A. 3 " " EVANS. L.W. 4 " " HALE. G.T. " ALLIM. J.E.	
	30/3/16		Training continued by section officers.	
	31/3/16		2nd Lt. G. LONDON reported for duty as transport officer. 3/2nd LONDON REGT.	

E.G.Salt
Capt.
O/C 115th Coy

Army Form C. 2118.

WAR DIARY
or
INTELLIGENCE SUMMARY
(Erase heading not required.)

Confidential

WAR DIARY.

115 MACHINE GUN COMPANY.

From 1st April 1916 to 30th April 1916

WAR DIARY or INTELLIGENCE SUMMARY

Army Form C. 2118.

Place	Date	Hour	Summary of Events and Information	Remarks and references to Appendices
Belton Pk. Grantham	1/4/16		Training of m.g. gunners continued.	
	10/4/16		Mobilisation stores being drawn daily.	
			4 men reported for duty	
	10/4/16		2nd Lt. LEWIS. D.A. transferred to No 180 Coy.	
	11/4/16		" GIRVAN, A. reports for duty.	
	12/4/16		" " 2nd Roy. Scots Fus.	
	14/4/16		1 NCO + 2 Men transferred from the Company.	
			" JOHNSON. C.H. 16th KINGS LPL REGT reports for duty	
	16/4/16		16 men reported to the Coy, reported for duty.	
			10 Officers horses + 3 mules drawn.	
	19/4/16		2 men reported for duty	
	22/4/16		1 " " " "	
	23/4/16		1 " " " "	
	28/4/16		1 " " " "	
	1/30.4.16		Training of m.g. gunners carried on by the Officers of the Company with the assistance of Sergt Instructors, under the supervision of the Staff. Fitting of Harness + training of drivers + preparing transport for the road. Mobilisation stores being drawn daily.	
	15/30.4.16			

J.F. [signature]
Capt.
O/C 115th Bn. G. Coy.

Army Form C. 2118.

WAR DIARY
or
INTELLIGENCE SUMMARY
(Erase heading not required.)

Place	Date	Hour	Summary of Events and Information	Remarks and references to Appendices
Belton Pk Grantham	1/5/16 to 11/5/16		Preparing the Company for the road. Route marches with transport. Night operations & relief of trenches.	
	12/5/16		Company mobilised for service overseas. T.C. orders.	
	13/5/16		Issuing overseas kit and packing limbers.	
	14/5/16		do do do	
	15/5/16		Handing over barrack furniture &c. Clearing of huts &c. Handing over barrows, surplus to establishment.	

Army Form C. 2118.

WAR DIARY
or
INTELLIGENCE SUMMARY
(Erase heading not required.)

Confidential

War Diary
of
115 Machine Gun Company

From 1st May 1916 To 31st May 1916

Army Form C. 2118.

WAR DIARY
or
INTELLIGENCE SUMMARY

(Erase heading not required.)

Instructions regarding War Diaries and Intelligence Summaries are contained in F. S. Regs., Part II. and the Staff Manual respectively. Title Pages will be prepared in manuscript.

Place	Date	Hour	Summary of Events and Information	Remarks and references to Appendices
BELTON PARK.	16/5/16	1.0 a.m.	Company paraded outside "B" LINES guardroom.	5.
GRANTHAM.		2.15 A.M.	Marched off.	
		4.0 a.m.	Began entraining, completed 4.23 a.m.	
		2.0 p.m.	Arrived @ SOUTHAMPTON and detrained.	
		6.30 p.m.	The company with exception of the party mentioned below on board a smaller steamer ——— left about 7.30 p.m. (under Capt. Scott). All transport horses, mules, (4 officers & 141 men on S.S. "City of Benares"; left at 9.6 p.m.	
	17/5/16	4.0 a.m.	At SPITHEAD, fog delays the "City of Benares." Arrived HAVRE 1.30 p.m. Earlier party arrived 6.30 a.m.	
		6.0 p.m	Marched to the rest camp outside HAVRE. Under canvas.	
HAVRE.	18/5/16	11.0 a.m.	Received orders to move off.	
		2.30 p.m.	Marched to La Gare Marchandise, LE HAVRE.	
		5.0 p.m.	Entrained. Left @ 7.30 p.m.	
	19.5.16		En route, via Abbéville and St. Pol.	10.6.1

WAR DIARY
or
INTELLIGENCE SUMMARY
(Erase heading not required.)

Army Form C. 2118.

Place	Date	Hour	Summary of Events and Information	Remarks and references to Appendices
B.E.F.	19.5.16	2.0 p.m.	Arrived and detrained at LA GORGUE. Marched to billets at LE DRUMEZ, near LAVENTIE.	
LE DRUMEZ	20.5.16		Company engaged in cleaning of billets, cleaning and repacking of limbers.	
— " —	21.5.16		Company inspected by Brigadier General H.J. EVANS commanding 115 Infantry Brigade. Church parades.	
— " —	22.5.16	11.0 am	Inspection by Major General IVOR PHILIPPS, D.S.O. commanding 38th (WELSH) DIVISION.	
		2.0 pm	2/Lt: ALLIN, GIRVAN, SOUTHON and YEARDLEY with several N.C.O.'s & men go to No. 6. MOTOR MACHINE GUN BATTERY for instruction in neutralfire. Balance of company carried on with training.	
— " —	23.5.16		2/Lt: EVANS and HALE with 16 N.C.O.'s & men sent into the MOATED GRANGE sector for instruction under the Lewis gun officer. Severe bombardment between Winchester House and ERITH STREET.	
— " —	24.5.16		Company carried on with training. In evening received orders to move off to new billets at Les Puresbecques warned party in readiness and sent on party to M.M.G. Battery at MERVILLE.	

Army Form C. 2118.

No: 8

WAR DIARY
or
INTELLIGENCE SUMMARY

(Erase heading not required.)

Instructions regarding War Diaries and Intelligence Summaries are contained in F.S. Regs., Part II. and the Staff Manual respectively. Title Pages will be prepared in manuscript.

Place	Date	Hour	Summary of Events and Information	Remarks and references to Appendices
LE DRUMEZ.	26/5/16	9.0 am	Company leave billets & proceed to LES PURESBECQUES via ESTAIRES and MERVILLE. Take over billets and commence cleaning of same.	
LES PURESBECQUES	27/5/16		Commence 8 days REST. Programme, elementary from drill, advanced from drill, immediate action, to Route marches	
"	28.5.16		"	
"	29.5.16		Sunday, Church parades.	
"	30.5.16		Work as on 29.5.16, company training.	
"	31.5.16		do	

E.W.S.
Capt.
O.C. 115 M.G. Coy.

Army Form C.2118.

115 M G C
Vol 2

XXXVIII

WAR DIARY
or
INTELLIGENCE SUMMARY
(Erase heading not required.)

Confidential

War Diary
of
115 Machine Gun Company

From 1st June 1916. To 30th June 1916.

WAR DIARY
INTELLIGENCE SUMMARY

Army Form C. 2118.

No. X. 9

Place	Date	Hour	Summary of Events and Information	Remarks and references to Appendices
LES PURESBECQUES	June 1st 1916		Usual programme of rest training: 9.0 a.m. to 4.30 p.m.	
		9.0 p.m	Received orders to stand by ready to move off, enemy attacking	
		10.0 p.m	Orders received to stay down	
"	June 2nd		Company went to Divisional Gas School near LA GORGUE. All taken into chamber, free of chlorine gas, for demonstration.	
"	June 3rd		Company in training and preparing to leave.	
"	June 4th		Church parades at LESPURESBECQUES, MERVILLE and NEUF. BERQUIN.	
"	June 5th	7.45 a.m	2Lt: EVANS went to LAVENTIE, to take over billets.	
		9.0 a.m	Company leaves LES PURESBECQUES and proceeds to LAVENTIE via MERVILLE and ESTAIRES. Arrive @ 12. o'clock noon.	
		2.0. p.m	Company leaves to take over emplacements & posts in front of AUQUISSART Sector held by 114. MACHINE GUN COMPANY. (see MAP over leaf)	
		6.0 p.m.	2.LTS: EVANS and HALE go to NO: 5. MOTOR MACHINE GUN BATTERY for instruction in overhead fire.	DM

Army Form C. 2118.

WAR DIARY
INTELLIGENCE SUMMARY
(Erase heading not required.)

Place	Date	Hour	Summary of Events and Information	Remarks and references to Appendices

Fo. 8. 10.

Situation of Machine guns in "FAUQUISSART Sector".

- ☒ A.I. POST.
- ☒ MOUQUMENT. LITTOCK'S POST. 2 gns.
- ☒ FLANK POST.
- ☒ MASSELOT POST. (Taken from MASSELOT Ho. by day)
- ☒ FELON POST.
- ☒ FAUQUISSART POST.
- ☒ MASSELOT HOUSE. (2 gns.)
- ☒ ROAD BEND POST. (By day)
- ☒ C.R.A. POST. (by night)
- ☒ ELGIN POST.

Nº 8. Nº 6. Nº 3. Nº 2.

WAR DIARY or INTELLIGENCE SUMMARY

Army Form C. 2118.

No. 12.

(Erase heading not required.)

Place	Date	Hour	Summary of Events and Information	Remarks and references to Appendices
LAVENTIE	12th June 1916		2Lt. EVANS went on to ROBECQ to find Billets for company. Company left LAVENTIE and marched to ROBECQ, arrived about 1.0pm.	
ROBECQ	13th June		2Lt. EVANS and N.C.O sent on to find Billets for company at AUCHEL. Company rest, clean up & have Kit Inspection.	
ROBECQ	14th June	8.15 A.M.	Left ROBECQ and marched to AUCHEL via LILLERS. Billets scattered but very good.	
AUCHEL	15th June	6.0 am	March out of AUCHEL for CHELERS via FREVILLERS. Company arrived about noon at HERLIN-LE-VERT where fields there situated. Very team fields.	
HERLIN-LE-VERT	16th June		Company Training in Divisional Training area.	
"	17th		"	
"	18th June am		W.O. Inspection by General C. de la Hille, Brigadier of Makina Gen. companies.	
"	19th		Church parade in afternoon.	
"	20th		Coy. Training in Divisional Training area.	
"	21st		"	

Army Form C. 2118.

WAR DIARY
or
INTELLIGENCE SUMMARY
(Erase heading not required.)

Place	Date	Hour	Summary of Events and Information	Remarks and references to Appendices
LAVENTIE	5th June		Reliefs completed and emplacements visited	
"	6th June		"	
"	7th June		Company in trenches. No casualties	
"	8th June		"	
"	9th June		Received instructions through Divisional H.Q. to take over gun positions & quarters of No 5. M.M.G. Battery. This was done, and our morning places in position.	
"	10th June		Received orders to take over M.M.G. mountings (CLARKE-JARVIS) Last section of M.M.G. Battery left 2ND King's afraid. Notified that probably we were (relieved) on the 11th June. Made all arrangements. Eight mittens are supplied arms from Brigade	
"		8.30 P.M.	Took Brigade Major of 184th Brigade round our front line emplacements.	
"	11th June	1.0 P.M.	O.C. 106 M. & C.W. reported at H.Q. Proceed to take over gun positions in the line Reliefs not reported complete until dark owing to remain at LAVENTIE for the night	

2449 Wt W14957/M90 750,000 1/16 J.B.C. & A. Forms/C.2118/12.

Army Form C. 2118.

70. 12. 13.

WAR DIARY
or
INTELLIGENCE SUMMARY

(Erase heading not required.)

Instructions regarding War Diaries and Intelligence Summaries are contained in F. S. Regs., Part II. and the Staff Manual respectively. Title Pages will be prepared in manuscript.

Place	Date	Hour	Summary of Events and Information	Remarks and references to Appendices
HERUN-LE-VERT	22nd June 1916		Company Training (Tactical schemes) in Divisional Training area.	
— ,, —	23rd June		"	
— ,, —	24th June		Brigade Tactical scheme in training area.	
— ,, —	25th June		Divisional scheme	
— ,, —	26th June		Remained Iron rations (Divisional order).	
— ,, —	27th June	5.0 p.m.	Company engaged in packing & cleaning at Lindert. Paraded Marched out of CHELERS for BEAUVOIR via TINQUES and BONNIERS.	
BEAUVOIR	28th June	7.45 p.m.	Arrived at 3.0 a.m. Billets satisfactory. Men rested during morning and afternoon. Paraded and moved off at 8.0 p.m. Marched to LONGUEVILLETTE via GEZAINCOURT Arrived at billets 3.30 a.m. Great strain on pair limbers.	
LONGUEVILLETTE	28th/29th June	3.30 a.m.	Arrived. Billets satisfactory. Men rested all day.	
— ,, —	29th June		Carried on with company training and cleaning.	CJN

2449 Wt. W14957/Mgo 750,000 1/16 J.B.C. & A. Forms/C.2118/12.

WAR DIARY

INTELLIGENCE SUMMARY

(Erase heading not required.)

Army Form C. 2118.

No. 14.

Place	Date	Hour	Summary of Events and Information	Remarks and references to Appendices
LONGUEVILLETTE	June 30th 1916		Friday. Company engaged in clearing limbers & training during forenoon.	
		3.0 p.m.	Marched out of billets for GAZAINCOURT.	
		5.0 p.m.	Marched out of GAZAINCOURT for TOUTENCOURT. Halted from 8.0 p.m. — 10.0 p.m. outside BEAUQUESNE.	
	1/7/16	12.10 a.m.	Arrived TOUTENCOURT.	

O.H.

O.H.
Major
O.C. 115 M.G.C.y

115th Inf.Bde.
38th Div.

WAR DIARY

115th MACHINE GUN COMPANY.

J U L Y

1 9 1 6

WAR DIARY
or
INTELLIGENCE SUMMARY

Army Form C. 2118.

Confidential
War Diary
of
115 M.G. Coy.

From 1st July 1916
To 31st July 1916.

Army Form C. 2118.

No. 15

WAR DIARY
or
INTELLIGENCE SUMMARY
(Erase heading not required.)

Place	Date	Hour	Summary of Events and Information	Remarks and references to Appendices
	15/7/16	12.10 a.m.	Company arrived & took over billets @ TOUTEN COURT.	C.N.S.
TOUTEN- COURT	17/7/16	11.0 a.m.	Foot inspections.	
		2.0 p.m.	Cleaning of billets & issuing of stores.	
		6.0 p.m.	Company paraded for pay. Received orders to be ready to move at once.	
		7.0 p.m.	Billeting party reported at B'de H.Q. Received orders to be at spot 200 yards from market place on TOUTENCOURT — LEALVILLERS. ROAD at 9.30 P.M.	
		9.20	Join up with column, the 17th Batt. ROYAL WELSH FUSILIERS in front.	
		12.0 M.D.	arrived at ACHEUX. Transport brigades; company under airways in wood.	C.N.S.
ACHEUX.	2/7/16	a.m.	Sunday inspections.	
		p.m.	Guns limbers being cleaned & prepared for going into action & ready for company & the Heavy to move off without order received at night for company & the Heavy to move off without delay.	C.N.S.

Army Form C. 2118.

WAR DIARY
INTELLIGENCE SUMMARY
(Erase heading not required.)

Place	Date	Hour	Summary of Events and Information	Remarks and references to Appendices
ACHEUX	3/7/16	am	Inspection & Drill.	
		pm	Bathing.	
		4.0 pm	Received orders to stand to.	
		8.20 pm	Moved off for BUIRE–SUR–ANCRE via VARENNES.	O.W.
	4/7/16	3.0 am	Arrived BUIRE–SUR–ANCRE.	
BUIRE-SUR-ANCRE	5/7/16	am	Company resting.	
		1.90 pm	Moved to MAMETZ via MEAULTE, FRICOURT.	
			Arrived MAMETZ 4.45 p.m. Bivouaced for night. X.11.C.8.2. Map MONTAUBAN (57.2.N.E. ST.9.W. 1.20.000. (57.2.N.E. 62.N.W.)	
MAMETZ	6/7/16	pm	Resting. Company in reserve. Standing by to move into the line. Received orders to take up the following positions:–	J.W.R.
		5.0 pm	2 guns to CATERPILLAR WOOD (2nd Lt. Yeardley) to cover Eastern side of MAMETZ WOOD & ground between it & BAZENTIN–LE–GRAND WOOD. 4 guns (2nd Lts. Evans & Given) to high ground forward of WHITE TRENCH	

Army Form C. 2118.

WAR DIARY
INTELLIGENCE SUMMARY
(Erase heading not required.)

Instructions regarding War Diaries and Intelligence Summaries are contained in F.S. Regs, Part II. and the Staff Manual respectively. Title Pages will be prepared in manuscript.

p. 17

Place	Date	Hour	Summary of Events and Information	Remarks and references to Appendices
MAMETZ	6.7.16	5.0 P.M.	10 Remaining guns in Reserve in POMMIER'S REDOUBT	
		8 P.M.	Proceeded to trenches via CARNOY & THE LOOP to take up above positions	
	7.7.16	A.M. 3.30 Recon	Guns near WHITE TRENCH in position viz:- 3 guns in forward positions on open ground E. of WHITE TRENCH commanding MAMETZ WOOD (St E side) SUNKEN ROAD, FLAT IRON COPSE, SABOT COPSE & open ground East of MAMETZ WOOD. 1 gun in WHITE TRENCH covering SUNKEN ROAD & Southern edge of MAMETZ WOOD	
		7.45	Positions heavily shelled - no casualties	
		11.0	Guns moved forward to new positions on slope & covering fire on above Targets maintained during Infantry advance.	
		P.M. 9.30.	4 Guns from WHITE TRENCH positions withdrawn to POMMIER'S REDOUBT TOTAL casualties 7/7/16 - Killed 1 Wounded 2	KWE
	8.7.16	A.M. 2.30	2 Guns in CATERPILLAR WOOD withdrawn to POMMIER'S REDOUBT	
		5.0	all guns return to Bivouac.	
	9.7.16	3 P.M.	4 guns under 2/Lts. Southon & Davis take to old positions on commanding ground East of WHITE TRENCH. 2 Guns under 2nd Lt. Allan to MARLBOROUGH WOOD to cover open ground	KWE

2449 Wt. W14957/M90 750,000 1/16 J.B.C. & A. Forms/C.2118/12.

Army Form C. 2118.

WAR DIARY
INTELLIGENCE SUMMARY
(Erase heading not required.)

f. 18

Place	Date	Hour	Summary of Events and Information	Remarks and references to Appendices
MAMETZ (conTd)			Between BAZENTIN-LE-GRAND & MAMETZ WOOD also rt. flank of MARLBOROUGH WOOD. 2 Guns under 2nd Lieut Hale to CATERPILLAR WOOD to cover right edge of MAMETZ WOOD & ground between rt BAZENTIN-LE-GRAND & top & S. of MAMETZ WOOD in case of COUNTER ATTACK. 1 Gun in Reserve at Line H.P.	
10.7.16	3 A.M. 10 P.M	1 Gun Team put out of action in CATERPILLAR WOOD. Orders received that MAMETZ WOOD must be held at all costs. Following dispositions of guns made:— 4 Guns to Eastern side, 4 Guns to Western side of MAMETZ WOOD 1 in Reserve at Bde. H.Q. in MAMETZ WOOD. 2 Guns remaining in CATERPILLAR WOOD & 1 left in WHITE TRENCH all available men for Bivouac to assist in carrying Guns, Ammunition, &c to positions in MAMETZ WOOD.	
10.7.16 11.7.16	M.N.			
11.7.16	A.M 3.0	MAMETZ WOOD entered. 8 Prisoners taken 1 shot by Capt. ED Jnk. 12/Lt. A.M. Sorilan at S.E. corner of Wood.	MSR

Army Form C. 2118.

FO 19

WAR DIARY
INTELLIGENCE SUMMARY
(Erase heading not required.)

Instructions regarding War Diaries and Intelligence Summaries are contained in F.S. Regs., Part II. and the Staff Manual respectively. Title Pages will be prepared in manuscript.

Place	Date	Hour	Summary of Events and Information	Remarks and references to Appendices
MAMETZ	11.7.16	6 AM	Positions taken up in MAMETZ WOOD. 2 Guns advanced position E. side enfilading edge of wood (Map Reference S.13.D.50.50) and cooperating with 1 Gun at position on E. side (Map Ref. S.20.A.10.80.) 2 Guns at R.E. Strong Point W. encircling point on Railway line. (Map Ref. X.18.C. 05.25.) Covering left side of wood.	
			2 Guns S.W. corner of wood. (Map Ref. X.23.B.50.70.) 2 Guns in middle of wood. 1 Gun in reserve at Bde. Head Quarters. (Map Ref. X.18.C. 20.47.) 6 Casualties in Gun Teams of advanced positions on Eastern side of wood — believed from our Artillery Fire.	
		2.45 P.M.		
		3 PM	Infy. attack up wood Commenced and Guns were to receive positions as attack Guns withdrawn Forward of Infantry when heavy withdrew in accordance. Proceed from own Artillery Fire, with the exception of two on left flank and 1 on right flanks which maintained same positions. Suffered Heavy Shelling. Captain E.D. Job — O.C. Coy. — Killed by Shell at advanced position on West corner of wood, near railway line. Artillery relief by 32 M.G. Coy.	
		11.30 p.m.		

Casualties. 6/7/16 to 11/7/16
7.7.16. Killed 3 Wounded 12
10.7.16. " 1 " 16
11.7.16. " 4 " 10

(Sig.)

WAR DIARY
INTELLIGENCE SUMMARY
(Erase heading not required.)

Army Form C. 2118.

F. 20

Place	Date	Hour	Summary of Events and Information	Remarks and references to Appendices
MAMETZ	12.7.16	2.30 A.M.	22 M.G. Coy. arrives to relieve the Company.	
		2.30 P.M.	Coy. receives orders to entrain for ~~9pm~~ LONGPRÉ.	
		3.30 P.M.	SEC. LIEUT. JOHNSON shell shock Casualty.	
		4.30 P.M.	Transport leaves.	
		8.30 P.M.	Coy. receives orders to remain in bivouacs for tonight. Relief now complete.	
	13.7.16	5 AM	Coy. departs with Brigade to WARLOY- BAILLON via MÉAULTE, VILLE-SOUS-CORBIE, TREUX, BUIRE-SUR-L'ANCRE, RIBEMONT, BAIZIEUX in the following order:—	
			11th S.W.B.	
			10th S.W.B.	
			17th R.W.F.	
			16th Welsh	
			115 M.G. Coy.	
			115 T.M. By.	
			333 Coy. A.S.C.	
		8 AM	Transport joins Company at MÉAULTE.	
WARLOY BAILLON		1 PM	Arrive WARLOY- BAILLON.	
		7.30 PM	Company including Transport leaves for COUIN (men in motor lorries) via HEDAUDVILLE, FORCEVILLE, ACHEUX, LOUVENCOURT, and AUTHIE	
COUIN	14.7.16	11th	Arrive COUIN. Bivouac with Brigade.	
		10.16 AM	9 men to hospital	

C.J.H.

Army Form C. 2118.

WAR DIARY
or
INTELLIGENCE SUMMARY

(Erase heading not required.)

F.21

Instructions regarding War Diaries and Intelligence Summaries are contained in F.S. Regs., Part II. and the Staff Manual respectively. Title Pages will be prepared in manuscript.

Place	Date	Hour	Summary of Events and Information	Remarks and references to Appendices
COUIN	14.7.16	4 p.m.	Leave for COURCELLES-AU-BOIS arriving at 5 p.m. and take over part of trenches held by the 144th I.B. Bde. Machine Gun Company. Dispositions at COURCELLES J.29.B.35.80. Mine Guns put into the line two mornings two as follows:—	
COURCELLES AU-BOIS			No. 1. Fargate K.34.B.55.80.	
			" 2. Maitland K.34.B.34.95.	
			" 3. N.of Junction Worley+Hook R.29.C.00.80.	
			" 4. Junc. Crupier+Hook K.25.D.95.95.	
			" 5. S. Junction Esperance+Hook K.28.B.85.05.	Ref. Map. Hébuterne 57 D.N.E. 3+4. 1:10,000.
			" 6. S. Junction Cotton+Hook K.28.B.80.40.	
			" 7. Roland K.23.B.30.99.	
			" 8. Tournell Farm K.23.C.30.10.	
			" 9. Bessie Gun K.27.B.70.90.	
	17.7.16	10 A.M.	1 man to Hospital.	
		2 P.M.	Two missing men turn up, report for duty, also 2 civilians which went lost on MAMETZ-WARLOY-BAILLON road.	
	18.7.16	10 A.M.	1 man to Hospital.	
	20.7.16	1 PM	2 Infants M. Gunners arrive as Reinforcements.	
		1.30 p.m.	Pte. Francis discharged from Base Depot report as reinforcements.	
		3.30 P.M.	One man returns from hospital.	A.O.1186 of 1916 (Andrews).

2449 Wt. W14957/M90 750,000 1/16 J.B.C. & A. Forms/C.2118/12.

Army Form C. 2118.

F. 22.

WAR DIARY or INTELLIGENCE SUMMARY

(Erase heading not required.)

Place	Date	Hour	Summary of Events and Information	Remarks and references to Appendices
COURCELLES AU-BOIS	21.7.16	10 am	Reinforcements in the shape of attached men from the Battalions of the Brigade who have had no machine gun training report for duty: – 7 men from 16th Welch Regt. 6 men from 17th R.W.F. 6 men from 11th S.W.B. 8 men from 10th S.W.B. Total 27.	
		10 pm	Pte. Pirie (wounded) reports for duty again with Gas Army.	
	22.7.16		Enemy during night on communication trenches E. & W. of SERRE Enemy during night 21-22nd on (1) Cross Rds. K36. a 85.20 (3) K36 a 25.10 Sheep dip in orchard (4) German 3rd line (5) Trenches through SERRE (6) K36. a 70.90. (7) Main Rd. to SERRE.	GSA
			Relieved 2 men for Sim team with att attd (untrained) men. R.E.'s commence work on Emplacements 5 & 6 putting in new platforms Pte Tour goes to Hospital – shellshock. Reinforcement – 1 – (St. Pioneer) R.O. for water cart duties – from 13.7. 7. A. Inf R.	
	23.7.16		Mr. Yeandley relieves Mr. Swan One man from Hospital Caernarvonshire C.S.M. P. Healy reports for duty from 19 Bde M.S. Coy. (GHM) During 22/23 on German 2nd line trenches N. of SERRE (M.37 10 M 29). Inf R.	

2449 Wt. W14957/M90 750,000 1/16 J.B.C. & A. Forms/C.2118/12.

Army Form C. 2118.

F. 23.

WAR DIARY
INTELLIGENCE SUMMARY
(Erase heading not required.)

Instructions regarding War Diaries and Intelligence Summaries are contained in F. S. Regs, Part II. and the Staff Manual respectively. Title Pages will be prepared in manuscript.

Place	Date	Hour	Summary of Events and Information	Remarks and references to Appendices
COURCELLES AU-BOIS	24.7.16	11 am	2nd Lieut. Brian goes to Field Hospital. Draft of 35 men (including 2 Lance Corporals) all trained, report on arrival from Machine Gun Base Depôt as Reinforcements and are taken on the strength of the Company accordingly. Company now at full strength excepting 3 Officers. CASUALTIES – NIL.	
			Firing 23rd.–24th. on German 2nd. & 3rd. Lines in neighbourhood of SERRE.	
COURCELLES AU-BOIS	25.7.16	4pm 6 pm	Gun teams in front line relieved at 4pm. Is retired of 4 men per team. Relief complete. CASUALTIES – NIL.	
			Firing 23rd.–24th. on German 2nd. & 3rd. Lines near SERRE.	
COURCELLES AU-BOIS	26.7.16	4 p.m.	Capt. F.A.F. Bone (late 1/4. Devon Regt.) takes over command of the Company from the 26 m. innst. Capt. Knox-Little and 2nd. Lieut. A.C. Godding also posted to the Company and taken on strength accordingly. Names in full :— CAPTAIN FOSTER ALLAN FREDERIC BONE CAPTAIN WALTER LAWRENCE WOOD KNOX LITTLE SEC. LIEUT. ALBERT CHARLES GODDING	Coy. Commdr. 1st. Devons 9th Reserve Country 9/5 R.W.K. Rt. G.T.H.
			Firing 24th. – 25th. on German 2nd. and 3rd. Lines in neighbourhood of SERRE. CASUALTIES – NIL.	
			2nd Lieut. A. GIRVAN evacuated to No. 49 C.C.S.	
COURCELLES AU-BOIS	27.7.16		Firing night 26th.–27th. on German 2nd & 3rd Lines in neighbourhood of SERRE. Gun position at K23.b.30.99 having been heavily shelled during afternoon of 26th, also not open fire. Trench mountings were fired on positions K.23.b.30.99 K.28.b.Pt 05. K.29.b.75.80 CASUALTIES – NIL.	W.N.

2449 Wt. W14957/M90 759,000 1/16 J.B.C. & A. Forms/C.2118/12.

Army Form C. 2118.

WAR DIARY
or
INTELLIGENCE SUMMARY
(Erase heading not required.)

F 24

Place	Date	Hour	Summary of Events and Information	Remarks and references to Appendices
COURCELLES AU BOIS	28.7.16		During night 27-28th usual Fatigues in neighbourhood of SERRE. Relieved by 60th Machine Gun Company.	
		9 p.m.	Commenced relief 9 p.m., completed 11.40 p.m. CASUALTIES - NIL.	
LES-ARTOIS BUS-	29.7.16	12.45 p.m.	The Company left COURCELLES at 12.45 p.m. and marched to BUS-LES-ARTOIS	W/H
		2 p.m.	where it arrived at 2 p.m. Billeted in Huts in BUS wood.	
BUS-LES-ARTOIS	30.7.16	3.40 a.m.	1st Section left 15 pdr 10th S.W.B. and to march with them to BEAUVAL.	
		5.15 a.m.	2nd Section left 15 pdr 11th S.W.B. and to march with them to BEAUVAL.	
		5.45 a.m.	3rd Section left 6 pm 16th Welch ? to march with them to BEAUVAL.	
		6.30 a.m.	4th Section left 10 pm 17th RWF and to march with them to BEAUVAL.	
WULVERDINGHE	31.7.16		From the bivouac at BEAUVAL, each section left at different times and entrained at CANDAS for ST OMER.	n.30th
		6.30 a.m.	1st Section arrived	
		11 a.m.	2nd Section arrived	
		2.30 p.m.	3rd Section arrived	
		5 p.m.	4th Section arrived	
			Thus by 5 p.m. the whole Company was in billets at WULVERDINGHE.	W/H

Army Form C. 2118.

38/
115 M G C
Vol 4

WAR DIARY
or
INTELLIGENCE SUMMARY

(Erase heading not required.)

Confidential

WAR DIARY

115 MACHINE GUN COMPANY

From 1/8/16 — 1/9/16

Army Form C. 2118.

WAR DIARY
or
INTELLIGENCE SUMMARY
(Erase heading not required.)

F 25.

Instructions regarding War Diaries and Intelligence Summaries are contained in F. S. Regs., Part II and the Staff Manual respectively. Title Pages will be prepared in manuscript.

Place	Date	Hour	Summary of Events and Information	Remarks and references to Appendices
WULVERDINGHE	1.8.16	9.a.m.	A muster parade of the Company, a stock taken of all stores on hand. A good many differences found owing to loss in MAMETZ WOOD. During forenoon a thorough cleaning of all clothes etc.	
WULVERDINGHE	2.8.16	9.a.m.	Inspection of Gas Helmets, iron rations etc. During forenoon cleaning of stores etc. and repairing limbers.	W/d
		10.30am	Received orders from 115 Bde. that the Company will move at 4 a.m. tomorrow to BOLLEZEELE.	
		1.45p.m	2nd Lieut Hale & 2 men sent to BOLLEZEELE as billeting party.	
BOLLEZEELE	3.8.16	5.15 a.m.	Left WULVERDINGHE	
		7.15 a.m.	Arrived at BOLLEZEELE, where the whole Company is in billets.	
		7.p.m.	The Company rested during morning, in afternoon cleaned guns. Received instructions from 115th Brigade for training whilst in BOLLEZEELE area.	
BOLLEZEELE	4.8.16	6.30 a.m. 7-8 a.m. 9.15-10.15 10.30-11.30 11.45-12.15 3 p.m - 7 p.m.	Gun drill Close order infantry drill Physical drill Mechanism stoppages. Packing limbers.	

2449 Wt. W14957/M90 750,000 1/16 J.B.C. & A. Forms/C.2118/12.

Army Form C. 2118.

F.2b.

WAR DIARY
or
INTELLIGENCE SUMMARY
(Erase heading not required.)

Instructions regarding War Diaries and Intelligence Summaries are contained in F. S. Regs., Part II. and the Staff Manual respectively. Title Pages will be prepared in manuscript.

Place	Date	Hour	Summary of Events and Information	Remarks and references to Appendices
BOLLEZEELE	5.8.16		General training all day, including - Gun drill, Physical drill, Arobic horse drivien.	
-do-	6.8.16	6.30/6. 7.30am 9am.	Gun drill Church Parade	W.H.
-do-	7.8.16	9am/15 12 noon 3.30/4pm (10th Sept) 3pm-7pm	The baths at ZEGGERS CAPPEL were at the disposal of the Company. The men were marched there in 3 parties, leaving their billets at 6.30am, 7.30am & 6.10am. 2nd Lieut ALLIN taking 1st & 4th party. 2nd Lieut EVANS the 2nd & 2nd Lieut GODDING the 3rd. Reported the heat baths the Company have had so far. Cleaning, sorting stores in limbers, repacking limbers.	W.H. W.H.
-do-	8.8.16	6.30-8am 9.15-12.45 5-7pm	Close order drill, saluting drill Training in open warfare with Push animals. Care & cleaning.	W.H.
-do-	9.8.16	10am/15 1pm	The G.O.C. 115th Brigade inspected troth Company. Company's Transport. He then inspected the men's kit, and afk. that 2 wheel trawleys put the 1st Section through the Manual Drill; 2nd Lieut SOUTTON made the section (R.H.W.) come in & action from limbers; 2nd Lieut EVANS put the 3rd Section through	

2449 Wt. W14957/M90 750,000 1/16 J.B.C. & A. Forms/C.2118/12.

WAR DIARY or INTELLIGENCE SUMMARY

Army Form C. 2118.

F. 27.

Place	Date	Hour	Summary of Events and Information	Remarks and references to Appendices
BOLLEZEELE	9.6.16		Musketry; and 2nd Lieut. Hale lectured Offrs. & E. Section on "Discipline".	
		3 a.m.	The G.O.C. then inspected the billets, and when leaving expressed his satisfaction at the way the company worked.	
		5–7 p.m.	From Guns sent to Divisional H.Q. for overhauling. Immediate Action.	
			Received Corps orders that 2 new Lewis guns for the permanently attached to this company from the battalions. The primary duties of the Lewis gunners from each battalion, but they must be trained in Machine gunnery in accordance with store 24 men arrived from 10th & 11th S.W.B. and 16th Welch 8 from each battalion.	W.W.
–do–	10.6.16		Training all the morning, in cleaning Gun Drill. Physical Drill & instructors on 15 g.m.	
		3.30	In view of Company Sports tomorrow, a few heats were run off.	
		5–7	Immediate Action.	W.W.
–do–	11.6.16		Training all morning, including Musketry, Bayonet fighting, physical Drill & Gun Drill.	
		3.30 6 p.m.	Company sports – in which all the men took a keen interest. The Band of the 10th S.W.B. played.	

WAR DIARY or INTELLIGENCE SUMMARY

(Erase heading not required.)

Army Form C. 2118.

Place	Date	Hour	Summary of Events and Information	Remarks and references to Appendices
BOLLEZEELE	11.8.16		No. 11892. C.Q.M.S. Birkenshaw H.B. was remanded for 7.9.C.M., for disobeying an order and neglect of duty.	
-do-	12.8.16	6.30 - 12.30	In accordance with Corps orders 8 men arrived to be attached permanently from 17th R.W.F. This makes up the 32 men necessary for the 2 extra men per gun. ordered. Route march.	
		11 a.m. -1 p.m.		
	13.8.16	7-8 a.m. 10 a.m. 3 p.m.	Drill Church Parade. C.Q.M.S. Birkenshaw tried by 7.9.C.M. and acquitted of charges brought against him. 2nd Lieut EVANS and Cpl. Boyce left for Camiers tactical store and gunnery course under the Vickers gun.	
-do-	14.8.16		The usual daily training.	
-do-	15.8.16		The usual daily training, - including a tactical scheme for officers. Received information from Bde. that a 2nd Lieut. H.A. GARBUTT, 14th Royal Inn. would join the Company.	
-do-	16.8.16	10 a.m.	G.O.C. came round to inspect billets. Usual training all day.	

WAR DIARY
or
INTELLIGENCE SUMMARY

(Erase heading not required.)

Army Form C. 2118.

F.29

Place	Date	Hour	Summary of Events and Information	Remarks and references to Appendices
BOLLEZEELE	17.8.16		Rained all day	W.M. Stp
- do -	18.8.16		- do -	W.M.
BOLLEZEELE	19.8.16	11.45 p.m.	Received notice that O.C. shall proceed over the line tomorrow 19 inst. leaving Bde. H.Q. at 8.30 a.m.	
		5 a.m.	Received notice for Coy to be prepared tomorrow to take over the line, at 9 a.m.	
		8.30 a.m.	Sent one officer Mr Allen, bgr with Staff Captain to arrange relief.	
		8 a.m.	Received operation orders regarding taking over line from 12th Bde.	
		9.30 a.m.	The Company to proceed by train at 4.40 p.m. to POPERINGHE and thence by road to VLAMERTINGHE.	
		4.30 p.m.	Guns in limbers, and Transport left for POPERINGHE by road.	
		5.10 p.m.	Company entrained.	
		5.15 p.m.	Train left BOLLEZEELE for POPERINGHE.	
SHEET 28 N.W. A.23.c.6.8		10 p.m.	Arrived at POPERINGHE and commenced to march to VLAMERTINGHE	
		8.45	On march received orders not to take over from 12th M.G. Coy until tomorrow night. Headline to stay the night in Transport lines - sheet 28. A.23.c.6.8.	W.M.
- do -	20.8.16	10 p.m.	Arrived Transport lines Vlamertinghe.	
		7 a.m.	Advanced officer returned, having arranged for relief tomorrow at 10 p.m. He reports there are 13 guns the where in front, Support & Reserve lines and 3 guns at Coy. H.Q. (C.25.a.7.3.-C.21.c.1.2.) in Reserve. Relief arranged as follows:- 1 Section with 3 guns - under Mr Yearsley - take over Right Sector Position - 1. CROSS ROADS FARM - sheet 28.IV.W. C.22.c.3.3. - changed 6 months in B.18 Trench 2. THREADNEEDLE STREET - C.21.d.7.5 at C.22.C.1.1. 3. X.9 C.27.a.7.5.	

2449   Wt. W14957/M90 750,000 1/16 J.B.C. & A. Forms/C.2118/12.

Army Form C. 2118.

WAR DIARY
or
INTELLIGENCE SUMMARY

(Erase heading not required.)

Instructions regarding War Diaries and Intelligence Summaries are contained in F. S. Regs., Part II. and the Staff Manual respectively. Title Pages will be prepared in manuscript.

Place	Date	Hour	Summary of Events and Information	Remarks and references to Appendices
SHEET. 28 N.W. A.33.c.8.8	20.8.16	7.30	III Section - with 3 guns - under Mr Grabeling - to take over Centre Section.	
			Positions 4. HILL TOP FARM	
			5. VIEW FARM C.21.a.8½.8½	
			6. B.16.	
			IV Section with 4 guns - under Mr Hale - to take over Left Section.	
			Positions 7. FOCH FARM	
			8. LONE WILLOW C.20.b.4.0	
			9. KNARESBORO CASTLE C.21.a.6.1	
			10. CLIFFORD'S TOWER C.21.a.7.4	
			II Section with 3 guns - under Mr Swan - to take over Reserve Section.	
			Positions 11. WILSON'S FARM N	
			12. do E	
			13 CANAL BANK E	
		8/pm.	Company left for Coy. H.Qs. C.25.a.7.3 on Canal Bank, marching via ELVERDINGHE	
			DAWSON'S CORNER and BREMEN.	
		10.15/pm	Arrived at Coy. H.Qs. (C.25.a.7.3) Commenced relief	
Coy. H. Qs C.25.a.7.3	21.6.16	3.15am	Relief completed.	
			Night 20/21.15 - Quiet, no firing, no Casualties.	

Army Form C. 2118.

WAR DIARY
or
INTELLIGENCE SUMMARY

(Erase heading not required.)

Instructions regarding War Diaries and Intelligence Summaries are contained in F. S. Regs., Part II. and the Staff Manual respectively. Title Pages will be prepared in manuscript.

7.31.

Place	Date	Hour	Summary of Events and Information	Remarks and references to Appendices
Canal Bank C.15. a. 7.3 (Sheet 28. N.W.)	21.6.16	3 a.m. 5-5 p.m.	Artillery bombarded German lines.	
		7 p.m.	Gas Alarm given	
		7.45 p.m.	Gas Alarm — Gas Shell	
		10.15 – 11 p.m.	Gas Alarm — No Gas is either case occurred.	
			Quiet night.	
			Most of Machine gun positions are isolated, no inspection kept to them during daylight	
– do –	22.6.16		Quiet day.	
			It has been found that all the positions with exception of LONE WILLOW can be visited in daylight	
			Wiring night 22/23: from position B.13 to Cross roads near OBLONG FARM (C.16. b.6.3) from Threadneedle Street to Cross roads near BRIDGE HOUSE (C.24. a.2k.7½)	WAH
			Quiet night – No Casualties.	
– do –	23.6.16		Quiet day. Night 23/24 The wire position at "B.13" been worked on during night – 9 unspoiled	

2449 Wt. W14957/M90 750,000 1/16 J.B.C. & A. Forms/C.2118/12.

WAR DIARY or INTELLIGENCE SUMMARY

Army Form C. 2118.

7.32

Place	Date	Hour	Summary of Events and Information	Remarks and references to Appendices
Canal Bank C.25.c.7.3 (Sheet 28.N.W)	23/24		Firing:– From position i Theoretical Shoot on Cross Roads at C.24.c.0.0.5" Infantry is at present clear from position, on left of Sector, as trouble is being caused in a TURCO FARM machine gun in or near a strong Point WM. Casualties :– Nil.	
-do-	24th	3 p.m.	Relief Party started from Canal Bank. All positions relieved in daylight. Interception of LONE WILLOW, HILL TOP FARM & VIEW FARM.	
		9.30 p.m.	Total relief completed. The Officer in Left Sector has taken up his HQ at CLIFFORD FARM, from which place he can control fire at KNARESBORO CASTLE & CLIFFORD FARM.	
	24/25		Night firing:– From B.13 out at Cross Roads nr. OBLONG FARM – C.16.b.5.3 Theoretical Shoot at Road C.17.d.0.4. No Casualties.	
-do-	25th	2.30 p.m.	Divisional General came round. Visited WILSON'S FARM N.F.E.	

Army Form C. 2118.

WAR DIARY
or
INTELLIGENCE SUMMARY
(Erase heading not required.)

7.33

Place	Date	Hour	Summary of Events and Information	Remarks and references to Appendices
CANAL BANK C.25.a.7.5	25	7.30pm	Strong Points are being made at TURCO FARM – LA BELLE ALLIANCE – HILL TOP FARM. 2nd Lieut. RALPH STOCK 4/6 Suffolk Regt. reported for duty.	WW.
	25/26		Night firing. Work was again carried n/t on B.13 position for improvement. From Thornhurst Street front n.t Cross roads at C.24.d.85.	WW.
-do-	26th		No casualties. Quiet all day.	
	26/27		Night firing. From position at B.13 n at SPEY FARM – C.16.d.n.4 From Thornhurst Street n t Cross roads C.24.d.85. No casualties.	WW.
-do-	27th	4.30pm	First shells came over our position in X.9 Trench (C.27.a.2.5) – smashing in Men emplacement & the men's dug-out. – No casualties.	
	27/28		No firing done during night – as Battalions were relieving.	WW.
-do-	28th		A quiet day.	

Army Form C. 2118.

F. 34.

WAR DIARY
or
INTELLIGENCE SUMMARY
(Erase heading not required.)

Instructions regarding War Diaries and Intelligence Summaries are contained in F. S. Regs., Part II and the Staff Manual respectively. Title Pages will be prepared in manuscript.

Place	Date	Hour	Summary of Events and Information	Remarks and references to Appendices
CANAL BANK C 25. a. 7. 3.	28/11		Night, no firing on account of infantry relieving. No casualties.	JRL
"	29/11	7.45 AM	Received warning from Brigade H.Q. for alert. Wind S.E.	JRL
"	29/11	9.40 PM	Gas alarm. Everyone put on gas helmets & remained with them on for an hour, when the alarm was called off & we resumed out "the alert". No firing was carried out that night owing to infantry relief. No casualties.	JRL
"	30/11		Raining hard. Dugouts swimming in water. Some of the dugouts on the Canal Bank collapsed & working parties were detailed to repair. Carried out wire reconnais on German front line & support line from C 22 B 32 to C 23 c 07. No casualties.	JRL
"	31/11		Received very recent information that a gas attack is contemplated on our right by the 29 th Division & that though every arm brought front of Canal is to wear helmet on alert position. Rain has cleared off, had two hrs good work to do in repairing dugouts & employments.	JRL

Wilfred Parr
Cmmd 118 N.S. Co

2449 Wt. W14957/Mgo 750,000 1/16 J.B.C. & A. Forms/C.2118/12.

Army Form C. 2118.

WAR DIARY
or
INTELLIGENCE SUMMARY
(Erase heading not required.)

Vol 5

CONFIDENTIAL

115th Machine Gun Company

from 1st to 30th September

Army Form C. 2118.

WAR DIARY
or
INTELLIGENCE SUMMARY.
(Erase heading not required.)

Instructions regarding War Diaries and Intelligence Summaries are contained in F.S. Regs., Part II. and the Staff Manual respectively. Title pages will be prepared in manuscript.

4.35

Place	Date	Hour	Summary of Events and Information	Remarks and references to Appendices
Ennie Park C25.a.7.3	1/9/16	August 31st – 1st	Copy	
			The following firing was done from the positions in B.13 trench (C.22.c.11½) on to the Cross Roads near Oakey Farm from the junction in Thiepval 25 (C.21.d.53) on the Cross Road (C.17.d.0.4) near Chalks Wells on the left sector from Clifford's Jones (C.21.a.2.6) on to Kidney Wood and formidant line (C.10.d.75)	R.8
"	1/9/16 2 noon		In accordance with instructions in Divisional Defence Scheme rounds per gun were fired on various chosen ed known Well (C.26.c.92.1) and at Ovilliers (C.26.c.12)	R.8
"	"	2.30 am	Guns reported to have been laid off by 3rd Decuma Heavy has sustained any shift; 2nd have gun fired on some danger will also exception of the gun at Clifford's Tower which fired on Ovilliers they have answered and all	
		noon	R.8 (C.22.b.7.2)	R.8
			2nd actually	
	2/9/16	10.30 pm	Enemies gas alarm over account of	
		2.30 to 3.30 am	2.30 to 3.30 am gas alarm again no gas cover seen. All remained well behaved on during above time	
			Ray 2nd and Emmy from positions in B.13 trench on the Cross Roads (C.16.b.8.3) Gun position in Thiepval 25 on to Crow Roads (C24 d.0.5)	

Army Form C. 2118.

WAR DIARY
or
INTELLIGENCE SUMMARY.
(Erase heading not required.)

Instructions regarding War Diaries and Intelligence Summaries are contained in F. S. Regs., Part II. and the Staff Manual respectively. Title pages will be prepared in manuscript.

Y 36

Place	Date	Hour	Summary of Events and Information	Remarks and references to Appendices
Engl Redt C.25.a.7.3	Aug [1st]. 2nd		2nd (Canadian) Army relieved from Seaforth Tower on A. commenced relief of C.7. (C.16.b.5.6) up to date no casualties	R.8
	3/9/16		During morning Corps Commander visited Bgde HdQrs & side of Canal. Parties for tow were shown improvements in defences made since the Canal Bank at (C.25.b.0.8) & (C.25.b.1z.4) 2nd all day.	
	[date]		Hostile artillery was armed and from B.13 to the lyrium that was drawn from C.23.a.2.6 to C.23.c.6t.7½ also from Shrapnel. Sdm at X Roads near Bgde House at C.24.a.2½.7½ also from Seaforth Tower and lyr. his inundations at C.22.b.3.2. — C.23.c.0.7. Relieved at [time]	
	4/9/16		Corps Commander visited L Sector 4.30 a.m. Early morning our artillery 3.30 p.m. 2nd Canadians & hummed the Canadians covered of defences accomplish of options. Steve raising Jesuits on Real reorderdown Aug [4th]. 5th. & intense fire was carried out from Seaforth Tower on O House Y ... & our ammunition dump also blazed off (C.22.b.7.8) and 2nd Army Relief by 1114 to 6 Rd. 11.30 pm. 9 Canadians began to arrive at 7.30 pm. Relief completed 4.20 am.	
	5/9/16		Relief carried out successfully, a move to Machine Lyon Tavern	

Army Form C. 2118.

WAR DIARY
or
INTELLIGENCE SUMMARY.
(Erase heading not required.)

Place	Date	Hour	Summary of Events and Information	Remarks and references to Appendices
Canal Bank	Aug 5th		We reached 113th Inf Bde Cos & successfully carried out by 3 am	
C.19.c.3.6		4.00	Whilst there are 18 guns on the line placed at the following positions:-	
			I Right Group Positions	
			D.1 C.14.c.9.1	
			D.3 B.18.X.11 – C.14.c.3.4	
			N.1 C.19.b.9.4½	
			Y.1 Hassenfield Rd – C.19.b.3.8	
			The last position is the only one which can be safely approached in day time	
			II Left Group Positions	
			F.1 Bodd XVIII C.13.b.1.4	
			F.2 White Trench – C.13.a.7.8	
			P.1 Taupede C.7.c.2½.1½	
			F.3 Wajdth Cave C.7.c.2.3	
			all these positions can be approached in daylight	

T2134. Wt. W708–776. 500000. 4/15. Sir J. C. & S.

Army Form C. 2118.

4.3.8

WAR DIARY
or
INTELLIGENCE SUMMARY.
(Erase heading not required.)

Instructions regarding War Diaries and Intelligence Summaries are contained in F. S. Regs., Part II. and the Staff Manual respectively. Title pages will be prepared in manuscript.

Place	Date	Hour	Summary of Events and Information	Remarks and references to Appendices
East Bank C.19.c.3.6			III Signal Rendezvous	
			O.1 Szwank off Tu C.13.a.3½.½	
			O.2 W. Bank Canal C.13.a.3½.3	
			P.3 a — C.7.c.0.2	
			Z.1 Near Curlew Road — D.13 C.1.5	
			All these points can be approached defiladed the lad one Z.1 in	
			behind the Aix de Luc ridge commanded by the German trenches N.O.a	
			the ground was dry	
			IV Recon Raiders	
			X.1 C.19.a.14.21	
			X.2 C.19.a.2.3	
1/9/16	5 pm 6.30 pm	Today heavy shelling round Regt. Lator	
			One howitzer was mounted at D.3 garden	
		Night	Heavy firing from X.1 positions on trenches Roads at Chemin Etbouet	10 K.G.
do	2/9/16:		A good day	

T2134. Wt. W708—776. 500000. 4/15. Sir J.C. & S.

Army Form C. 2118.

WAR DIARY
or
INTELLIGENCE SUMMARY.
(Erase heading not required.)

Instructions regarding War Diaries and Intelligence Summaries are contained in F. S. Regs., Part II. and the Staff Manual respectively. Title pages will be prepared in manuscript.

7. 39

Place	Date	Hour	Summary of Events and Information	Remarks and references to Appendices
Cross Roads C.9.c.3.6	8th to 9th Sept		Enemy drew X.I pontoon on the Cross Roads at C.9.d.0.2	
			" N.I " " " " at C.9.d.3½.4½	
			" F.3 " " " " German dug out road & railway	
			In the early morning the Germans advanced over several rifle grenades surrounding 2 men — one only slightly who returned to duty. 2nd Lieut R Steele left on transport at 10.40 m.9.80	W.K.C.
	9/9/16		A quiet day. 2 new pontoons were shown to mined fire in 4 yards at C.13.c.3½.8½ & C.13.a.3½.7.	
	9th–10th Sept		Enemy's guns down from X.I. Pontoon on the Cross Roads at C.9.d.10. No casualties.	
	10/9/16		Firing transferred of 10 AC – 11 AC X.I. pontoon on the Cross Roads at C.15.b.3.4½	
	10 to 11th Sept		Our Cavalry during night - wounded 11 AC – 12 AC Enemy during night	W.K.C.
	11/9/16		From O.1 pontoon on the Rickew Cross Road C.2.c.9½	
			" N.I " " Cross Roads C.9.d.3½.7½	
			" X.I " " Road at C.15.b.3.4½	

Army Form C. 2118.

WAR DIARY
or
INTELLIGENCE SUMMARY.
(Erase heading not required.)

7.4.0

Place	Date	Hour	Summary of Events and Information	Remarks and references to Appendices
Trench North C.19.c.3.6	11/9/16		During night the 2 new open positions nr Tirgade were completed	W.K.C.
	12/9/16		Position at F.3 improved during day. The parapet between F.2 & F.3 was friendly known in. The dug out at F.3 was also strengthened. Timing night 12th & 13th	
			From O.1. positions on to Peckau drawing C.2.c.9.8.	
			" N.1. " " Roads C.10.c.3.6½	
			" X.1. " " Cross Roads at C.9.d.0.2.	
	13/9/16		Received reinforcements from Base & Larges at 9.15 am	
			Dug out at posn X.1 improved during day & roof boarding put down. Timing night 13th – 14th.	
			From O.1. Trans'y fire on Peckau	W.K.C.
			" X.1. On de Road at C.15.c.3.4½	
	14/9/16 5.30pm		The emplacement at N.1 was improved during night	
	7.40pm		Artillery bombarded German lines & artillery fire ceased	

WAR DIARY or INTELLIGENCE SUMMARY.

Army Form C. 2118.

Place	Date	Hour	Summary of Events and Information	Remarks and references to Appendices
Cane Post C.19.c.3.6	14/4/16	5.30 pm	Machine gun fire opened from following positions	7.4.1.
			O.1. order ground around Redan & between bearing 43° & 55° mag	
			N.1. " " Road at C.10.c.3.6½	
			X.1. " "GooRoad" C.7.d.o.2	
			Our Infantry ordered medical search at "morning" from front (C.13.c.3½.8½.) line from Kny't farm to High Command Redoubt. The enemy evidently somewhat unsettled as nothing got up and at 12.30 pm found that no attempt had been made by the Germans to man the wire and by the artillery in the afternoon	
			C.13.c.3½.7. Undress annihilating from C.14.a.6.8 to C.9.c.3.4.	
	15/4/16	12.25 am	All machine guns from ourselves as nothing systems were and and no reaction	
		2 am	Machine gun fire again opened as previously	w.G.K
		3.15 pm	Artillery bombarded of front line	
		do 5.15 pm	Germans replied and got sufficient at F3 and blown in, burying men & guns. The remainder of gun not damaged Guns from F2 were withdrawn	

Army Form C. 2118.

WAR DIARY
or
INTELLIGENCE SUMMARY.
(Erase heading not required.)

Instructions regarding War Diaries and Intelligence Summaries are contained in F. S. Regs., Part II. and the Staff Manual respectively. Title pages will be prepared in manuscript.

Place	Date	Hour	Summary of Events and Information	Remarks and references to Appendices
Zouave Bank				
C.19.a.3.6	15/9/16	8.30pm	Reliefs from rear done	
			From C.13.c.3½.8½ in do figures to line from Kupp farm to High Command Redout	
			" C.13.c.3½.7 from C.14.a.2.6 to C.9.c.3.4	
			" X.1 Reld at C.15.b.3.4½	
			" O.1 lynes round Pilckem	
			" N.1 Reld at C.10.c.3.6½	
		11pm to 12.8 am	Artillery Contacted Aymero lines. Enemy mig'd expecting at F.3. line repaired.	
			No reaction	
	16/9/16		Enemy drawing Arty 16th-17th	
			From O.1 or do Red. C.1.b.9.6	
			" X.1. " Red C.9.d.0.2	
	17/9/16	7.45pm	Relief commenced by 11346 Machine gun Coy.	W.K.C.
	18/9/16	2am	Relief completed no Casualties	
		3.15 am	Arrived at "S" Camp A.22.d.9.3	
"S" Camp	14/9/16		During morning an reduction of latrines to find and reference	
A.22.d.8.3				

Army Form C. 2118.

743

WAR DIARY
or
INTELLIGENCE SUMMARY.
(Erase heading not required.)

Place	Date	Hour	Summary of Events and Information	Remarks and references to Appendices
S. Camp A.2.D.8.3	19/9/16	6.30 pm	5 men Rumer reported for duty from Base.	w. K. R.
	20/9/16		2nd Card allow and to Hospital.	w. K. C.
	21/9/16		Chemy Camp dropped for Horse Standings. Work carried out on Horse Standings	w. K. C.
	22/9/16	3 pm	Inspection of Brigade at E. Camp by Commanding II Army	
		4 pm	2nd Card Men of 1st returned from Leave of absence by Inauguration at Cairo	
			The area of no 142 Battens were increased	
	23/9/16	10.20 am	Men of 3 & 4 Sections were inspected	w. K. C.
			new ordered newaitaby for Horse Standings	
	24/9/16	11 am	Church Parade, Service held at Church Army Hut	w. K. C.
	25/9/16	8-11 am	Battle + wounded of Coy. worked	w. K. C.
	26/9/16		worked in Horse Standings	
			ad myld 2 Gubers of NCC's Roys from Base for Horse Standings	w. K. C.
	27/9/16		Special workingparties for Horse Standings of 16 NCO's + 1 rd Coy R E	
			2nd Card Musem worked from Base for duty	w. K. C.
	28/9/16		Same working parties as yesterday	w. K. C.

Army Form C. 2118.

WAR DIARY
or
INTELLIGENCE SUMMARY.
(Erase heading not required.)

Place	Date	Hour	Summary of Events and Information	Remarks and references to Appendices
Camp S	28 & 29/9/16		Somme by yesterday appeal	w K G
			Lecture schedule approved for young Officers	w K G
	30/9/16		Some working parties applied	w K G

Army Form C. 2118.

WAR DIARY
or
INTELLIGENCE SUMMARY

(Erase heading not required.)

J 36

Place	Date	Hour	Summary of Events and Information	Remarks and references to Appendices
CANAL BANK C.25.a.7.3		Night 2nd-3rd (cont'd)	Enemy was seen from Clifford Tower on to communication trenches near Colony Farm. (C16 B.0.6). Up to date no casualties.	
"	3/9/16	During morning	Corps Commander visited Right Sector of Line. Further positions were chosen where emplacements can be made on the Canal Bank at (C 25. B.0.8) & (C 25. B 1½.4). Quiet all day.	
		Night 3rd-4th	Enemy was carried on 1 June B.13 on to Jenner Shrine, Temporary from C.23.a.2½.6 to C.23.c.6½.7½. Also from Strafweth St. on to Friends near BRIDGE HOUSE at C.2.4.a.2½.7½. Also from Clifford Tower on to Jenner line morning Relief at C.22.d.3.2, C.23.c.0.7.	
	4/9/16		Corps Commander visited (a) Sector 4.30 A.M. Enemy shelling morning 2nd Louthen & Jenner went to Carrier on same configuration serving working 2nd Louthen & Jenner trenches in new condition. Shell cannot; trenches in condition.	
		Night 4/5	We relieved there was carried out from Clifford Tower (C.22 & 7.8.) to communication trench behind it, (C.22 & 7.8.) 9 communication trenches behind it, cleaned at 10.30 A.M. & trucks & two lorries left at 4.30	
	5/9/16		Quiet day. Relief by 114 M.G Coy returned to MACHINE GUN F.M. AM. Relief carried out successfully & returned to MACHINE GUN F.M. 9 successfully carried out by 3 A.M. 7/9/16	
	6th	Night 6/7th	We relieved 113 Heavy S Coy 9 successively carried out by 3 A.M. 7/9/16	
CANAL BANK C.19.e.3.6	7th	7th	There are 14 guns in the line, placed at the following positions —	

Army Form C. 2118.

WAR DIARY
or
INTELLIGENCE SUMMARY
(Erase heading not required.)

Instructions regarding War Diaries and Intelligence Summaries are contained in F. S. Regs., Part II. and the Staff Manual respectively. Title Pages will be prepared in manuscript.

Place	Date	Hour	Summary of Events and Information	Remarks and references to Appendices

CANAL BANK C.19.c.8.6	7/10 37		I. Right group Positions.
			    D.1. — C.14.c.5.1
			    D.3. BUTT XII — C.14.c.3.4
			    N.1. — C.19.c.9.4½
			    Y.1. — HUDDERSFIELD ROAD — C.19.c.3.8
			    The last position is the only one which can be safely approached in the day time.
			II. Left group Positions.
			    F.1. BUTT XVIII — C.13.b.1.4
			    F.2. WHITE TRENCH — C.13.a.7.8
			    P.1. FARGATE — C.7.c.2½.4½
			    F.3. WYATT'S LANE — C.7.c.2.3
			    All these positions can be approached in day light.
			III. Support Positions.
			    O.1. SZWAAN HOFF FM. — C.13.a.3½.4
			    O.2. W. BANK CANAL — C.13.a.3½.3
			    P.3.a. — C.7.c.0.2
			    Z.1. NEAR LIAISON POST — B.12.C.4.1
			    All these positions can be approached in day light; the truss on Z.1. to behind the French lines, is connected by Telephone with Brigade H.Q., who give notice re from.
			IV. Reserve Positions.
			    X.1. — C.19.a.1½.2½
			    X.2. — C.19.a.2.3	

2449 Wt. W14957/M90 750,000 1/16 J.B.C. & A. Forms/C.2118/12.

Army Form C. 2118.

WAR DIARY

INTELLIGENCE SUMMARY

(Erase heading not required.)

Instructions regarding War Diaries and Intelligence Summaries are contained in F. S. Regs., Part II. and the Staff Manual respectively. Title Pages will be prepared in manuscript.

7.38

Place	Date	Hour	Summary of Events and Information	Remarks and references to Appendices
CANAL BANK C.19.C.3.6	6/9/15 7/15	5 p.m. 6.35 p.m.	Fairly heavy shelling round Right Redr. One man killed + one wounded at D.3 position.	
-do-	N.I.L 7/8/15		Firing from X.1 position on t Cross Roads at CHEMINS ESTAMINET. A quiet day	W/W
-do-	8/9/15		Firing from X.1 position on t Cross Roads at C.9.d.0.r. N.1. " " " " at C.9.d.3½.4½ F.3 " at German Sap at point thankrange. In early morning the Germans sent over several rifle grenades, wounding 2 men - one at Lt Ch. p.tt, who retired slightly. 2nd Lieut R STOER left on Course to 10th M.G. Coy. A quiet day - 2 new positions were chosen for indirect fire - in FARGATE at C.13.e.3½.8½ + C.13.e.3½.7.	W/W
-do-	9/15		Firing was done from X.1 position on t Cross Roads at C.9.d.0.r. No casualties	W/W
-do-	9/10/15			
-do-	10/15		Firing done night 9/10/15 X.1 position on t Cross Roads at C.15.b.3.4½	W/W

Army Form C. 2118.

WAR DIARY
or
INTELLIGENCE SUMMARY
(Erase heading not required.)

F. 3. 9

Place	Date	Hour	Summary of Events and Information	Remarks and references to Appendices
CANAL BANK C.14.c.3.6	10/11		One Casualty during night — wounded	
-do-	11th		Firing during night 10/11th. From O.1. bearing n to PILCKEM Cross Roads C.2.c.9.8. " N.1. " " " Cross Roads C.9.d.3½.7½. " X.1. " " " Road at C.15.b.3.4½. During night the 2 new open trenches = FARGATE Mine Completed	
-do-	12th		Position at F.3 improved during day. The parapet between F.2 & F.3 is frequently blown in. The dug-out in F.3 was also strengthened. Firing night 12/13th From O.1. bearing to PILCKEM – Xroads C.2.c.9.8. " N.1. " " " Roads at C.10.c.5.6½ " X.1. " " " Cross Roads at C.9.d.0.2.	

Army Form C. 2118.

WAR DIARY or INTELLIGENCE SUMMARY
(Erase heading not required.)

Z.40

Place	Date	Hour	Summary of Events and Information	Remarks and references to Appendices
CANAL BANK C.14. C.3.b	13th		Received reinforcement from Base — 2 Corporals and 15 men.	
			Dug out at position X.1 improved during day. 1 floor traverse had blown.	
			During night 13th/14th.	W.W.
			from O.1. Traversing fire on PILCKEM.	
			" X.1. on to Road at C.15. c.3.4.4.	
			The emplacement at N.1 was improved during night.	
	14th	5.30pm	Artillery bombarded German lines	
		7.40pm	Artillery fire ceased.	
		8.30pm	Machine gun fire opened from following positions	
			O.1. — on to front around C.10.c.3.6.4.	
			N.1. — on to Road at C.10.c.3.6.4.	
			X.1. — on to Cross tracks at C.9.d.0.2.	
			New Emplacement — Indirect vertical searching Traversing German front line from C.13.c.3.4.6.4.	
			KRUPP FARM to HIGH COMMAND REDOUBT. This was evidently successful as raiding party going out at 12.30 a.m. found that no attempt had been made by the Germans to repair the wire cut by the Artillery in the afternoon.	
			C.13.c.3.4.7. Vertical searching from C.14.a.5.5 to C.9.c.3.4.	

Army Form C. 2118.

WAR DIARY
or
INTELLIGENCE SUMMARY
(Erase heading not required.)

Instructions regarding War Diaries and Intelligence Summaries are contained in F.S. Regs., Part II. and the Staff Manual respectively. Title Pages will be prepared in manuscript.

7.41.

Place	Date	Hour	Summary of Events and Information	Remarks and references to Appendices
CANAL BANK C.19.c.3.6.	15th	12.25 am	All machine gun fire ceased, no raiding parties were sent out.	
		2 am	Machine gun fire again opened, as previously. No casualties.	
		3.15 pm to 5.10 pm	Artillery bombardment of German line. 2 emplacements. German replied 9 dug-outs at F.3 were blown in, burying men & gun. No casualties. Gun & dug-out damaged. Team from F.2 was withdrawn. Following firing was done from C.13.c.3½.8½. on to German front line from KRUPP FARM to HIGH COMMAND REDOUBT	
		8.30 pm to Midnight	" C.13.a.3½.7 from C.14.a.5.6 & C.9.c.3.4 " X.1 Road at C.15.b.3.4½ " O.1 Round PILCKEM " N.1 Road at C.10.c.3.6.½	
		11 pm to 12.8 am	Artillery bombarded German line. Enemy light emplaced at F.3. was repaired.	

Army Form C. 2118.

WAR DIARY
or
INTELLIGENCE SUMMARY
(Erase heading not required.)

Instructions regarding War Diaries and Intelligence Summaries are contained in F.S. Regs., Part II. and the Staff Manual respectively. Title Pages will be prepared in manuscript.

Place	Date	Hour	Summary of Events and Information	Remarks and references to Appendices
CANAL BANK C.19.C.3.6	16th		Firing during night 16/17th. From O.1 on to Rivet C.1.f.8.6. " X.1 " " Cross Roads C.7.d.0.2.	W.H.
	17th	9.45 p.m.	Relief Commenced by 113th Machine Gun Company.	W.H.
	18th	2 a.m.	Relief Completed. — No Casualties.	W.H.
"S" Camp A.22.d.8.3		3.45 a.m.	Arrived at "S" Camp — A.22.d.8.3	W.H.
	19th		During morning inspection of kits etc. 5 found not up to requirements. 8 men drivers reported for duty from Base. 2nd Lieut ALLIN sent to Hospital.	W.H.
	20th	6.30 p.m.	Cleaning Camp — digging etc. for Horse Standings.	W.H.
	21st		Work carried out on Horse Standings.	W.H.
	22nd	3 p.m.	Inspection of Brigade at E Camp by G. Commanding II Army. 2nd Lieut Sexton partly relieved from Course of machine gun Instruction at Camiers.	W.H.
	23rd	10.20 a.m.	The men of No 1 & 2 Sections were inoculated. Non-inoculated men working on Horse Standings. Men of 3rd Sections were inoculated later working on Horse Standings	W.H.

Army Form C. 2118.

WAR DIARY
or
INTELLIGENCE SUMMARY
(Erase heading not required.)

7 4 3

Place	Date	Hour	Summary of Events and Information	Remarks and references to Appendices
Camp "S"	24/9/16	11.am	Church Parade. Service held at Church Army Hut.	WM
	25/9/16	8-11	Baths – remainder of Company inoculated	WM
	26/9/16		Work done on Horse Standings	
			At night 8 lorries of rubble brought from BRIELEN	WM
	27/9/16		Supplied working parties for Horse standings of 1 b: I: hold + Field Coys 25.	WM
			2nd Lieut Marles. W. reported from leave for duty.	
	28/9/16		Same working parties supplied.	
	29/9/16		Same working parties supplied.	WM
			Tactical scheme of Major Baldwin for young officers	
	30/9/16		Same working parties supplied.	WM

J.W. Browne Major
Comm 115th M.C.

2449 Wt. W14957/M90 750,000 1/16 J.B.C. & A. Forms/C.2118/12.

Army Form C. 2118.

Vol 6

WAR DIARY
or
INTELLIGENCE SUMMARY
(Erase heading not required.)

Folio 44 – 56

Confidential

115 Machine Gun Coy

from 1st to 31st October 1916.

McBryan
2/Lt

Army Form C. 2118.

F 4 4

WAR DIARY
or
INTELLIGENCE SUMMARY
(Erase heading not required.)

Instructions regarding War Diaries and Intelligence Summaries are contained in F.S. Regs, Part II. and the Staff Manual respectively. Title Pages will be prepared in manuscript.

Place	Date	Hour	Summary of Events and Information	Remarks and references to Appendices
Camp "S" A22.d.8.3.	1/10/16	11 AM 11:30	C of E Parade service in Church Army Hut. Nonconformist Parade Service at Bgn. H.Q.	R.W.A.
	2/10/16	6.30 P.M.	Raining heavily. Preparations for Relief of 114 M.G.C. 6 Guns sent to Canal Bank to be ready for early relief on 3/10/16	M.S.B.
	3/10/16	2 P.M.	Weather good. Teams for 6 Guns left "S" Camp for CANAL BANK to take up positions at KNARESBORO' CASTLE CLIFFORD'S TOWER HILLTOP FARM VIEW FARM B16 B13 The relief to take place as soon as possible	
		5 PM	Remainder of company left Camp "S" proceeded to CANAL BANK	
		7.30 PM	Relief of 114 M.G.Coy commenced. In addition to above positions taken up at: Threadneedle ST X 9 FOCH FARM LONE WILLOW STIRLING LANE (2) ENGLISH FARM WILSON FARM N. WILSON FARM E	

Army Form C. 2118.

F. 45

WAR DIARY
or
INTELLIGENCE SUMMARY

(Erase heading not required.)

Instructions regarding War Diaries and Intelligence Summaries are contained in F.S. Regs., Part II. and the Staff Manual respectively. Title Pages will be prepared in manuscript.

Place	Date	Hour	Summary of Events and Information	Remarks and references to Appendices
CANAL BANK	3/10/16	11.30 PM	Relief of 114 M.G. Coy complete. Three Officers & Machine Guns at CONEY ST. (SHQ) & 2nd Lt. GODDING at THREADNEEDLE ST. Lieut HALE & 2nd Lt SOUTHON C.O. 2nd in Command and 2/Lts. EVANS, DAVIS & MAILER at Coy. H.Q. CANAL BANK.	M.y.8
	4/10/16		No firing over night 3-4th. No Casualties. 2nd Lt. J.D. Allen struck off strength in Part II orders having been evacuated To England from C.C.S.	M.y.8
	5/10/16		Firing on night 4-5th — 3000 rds. From STIRLING LANE 'B' position - Target PILCKEM ROAD. C.8.c.8.5 to C.2.c.8.3 } 2000 rds	
			" " X.Rds. VON HUGEL FARM C.23.c.9.6 & BRIDGE HOUSE C.24.a.1.7. } 1000 rds	
		"	" THREADNEEDLE ST.	
		3.30 PM	MAJOR F.A.F. BONE proceeded on Special leave to ENGLAND. CAPT. W.L.W. KNOX-LITTLE left to join 57 M.G.C. 2nd Lt. L.W. EVANS takes over Temporary Command of Company from MAJOR BONE.	M.y.8

Army Form C. 2118.

F. 46

WAR DIARY
or
INTELLIGENCE SUMMARY
(Erase heading not required.)

Place	Date	Hour	Summary of Events and Information	Remarks and references to Appendices
CANAL BANK	6/10/16		During during night 5th/6th STIRLING LANE 'B'. 1500 yds Target PILCKEM RD. " " 500 " Enemy front line C.14.d.8 & working party on parapet. WREADNEEDLE ST. 2500 Rds Targets: - X Rds. Von Hugel Farm C23.c.9.6 (C.27.c.14.6) & Road at Bridge House C14.a.1.7. WH2	

	7/10/16		During during night 6th/7th
			                  Position Rds
			 STIRLING LANE 'B' 2000 TARGET
			 THREADNEEDLE ST. 2500 PILCKEM ROAD
			      X.9 1500 X.Rds. Von Hugel Farm C23.c.9.6
			 (C.27.a.8.3) Road at Bridge House C14.a.1.7
			                                                  Road Oblong Farm C.16.b.3.9 to
			                                                   C.16.b.9.4.	

		7.30 P.M.	Relief of 10 Gun Teams commenced B.16 B.13 KNARESBORO' CASTLE CLIFFORD'S TOWERS	

Army Form C. 2118.

F. 47

WAR DIARY
or
INTELLIGENCE SUMMARY.
(Erase heading not required.)

Place	Date	Hour	Summary of Events and Information	Remarks and references to Appendices
CANAL BANK	7/10/16		VIEW FARM	
			WILSON'S FARM N.	
			ENGLISH FARM	
			STIRLING LANE 'A'	
			" " B	
			HILL TOP FARM	
			2nd Lt MAILER relieved LIEUT. HALE at CONEY ST.	
		10.30 PM	Relief completed.	
		8 PM	T/Lt. BOUGHEY W.T. (MIDDX. REGT.) 103 M.G.C reported for duty as Second in Command.	MR
			Firing during night 7/8th	
	8/10/16		Position	Rds
			STIRLING LANE 'B'	2000
			THREADNEEDLE ST.	2000
			TARGET	
			PILCKEM ROAD	
			Road C23.a.6.5 Traceout To VON HUGEL FARM	
			Xrds C23.a.9.6	
			BRIDGE HOUSE Rd C24.a.1.7	MR

Army Form C. 2118.

F 48

WAR DIARY
or
INTELLIGENCE SUMMARY.
(Erase heading not required.)

Place	Date	Hour	Summary of Events and Information	Remarks and references to Appendices
CANAL BANK	8/10/16	11 AM	C. of E. Service CANAL BANK	
		11:30	Nonconf Service " "	
			Firing during night 8 – 9 L	
			Position	Rounds fired	Target
			Clifford Towers	200	Oblong Farm & X roads C22 & 95.10
			Stirling Lane "B"	225	Pilckem Road
			Threadneedle III	130	Pickelhaube House & House Zop Farm
			X 9 (C.27.a.8.3)	100	Oblong Farm Pt 6 C16 & 9.4	PTS
	9.10.16	9.30 pm	2/Lt Yendley returned from leave to U.K.	
			Firing during night 9-10 Ct	
			Position	Rounds fired	Target
			Stirling Lane "B"	220	Pilckem Road
			Clifford Tower	200	C.16.7.2 & C12 & 95.6
			Threadneedle 23	200	Pickelhaube House & House Zop Farm
			B.13 (C.27.a.1.1)	100	Juliet Farm (C17 a 9.4) & PTS. Craties Inouch (C17 5.2)

Army Form C. 2118.

F. 4. 9.

WAR DIARY
or
INTELLIGENCE SUMMARY.
(Erase heading not required.)

Instructions regarding War Diaries and Intelligence
Summaries are contained in F. S. Regs., Part II.
and the Staff Manual respectively. Title pages
will be prepared in manuscript.

Place	Date	Hour	Summary of Events and Information	Remarks and references to Appendices
CANAL BANK	10.10.16	10 a.m.	2/1st Lt Evans relieved 2/Lt Godding in trenches	
			1/2Lt Yeatley assumed command of No. 1. Section in trenches	
			Firing during night 10/11 G	
			Target	Rounds
			Gun	
			Stirling Lane "B"	Pilckem Rd.	2.0.0.
	11.10.16	6 p.m.	2/Lt Shell relieved 2/Lt Hales at CONEY ST.	
			Firing during night 10/12 G	
			Target	Rounds
			Gun	
			X. 9	Front line mine crater from C.22.a.1.7.6	1.1.0.0
			Stirling Lane "A" } C.22.a.1.9b to keep open a gap preparatory to a raid	1.5.0.0
			Stirling Lane "B" } Pilckem Road	2.0.0.0
	12.10.16		Firing during night 12-13 G	
			Target	Rounds
			Gun	
			CLIFFORD TOWERS } front line units C.22.A.1.8	5.5.0.0.
			STIRLING LANE "B" }	
			X.9		
			STIRLING LANE A	CANADIAN FARM	1.5.0.0
			FUGH FARM	X Roads C.9.d.3?	2.7.0.0
			THREAD NEEDLE ST	C.15.6.6.	

T2134. Wt. W703-776. 500000. 4/15. Sir J. C. & S.

WAR DIARY or INTELLIGENCE SUMMARY.

Army Form C. 2118.

F S·O

Place	Date	Hour	Summary of Events and Information	Remarks and references to Appendices
CANAL BK.	13.10.16		Firing during night 13-14th — on Potizeon Rd. — 2·000	
	14.10.16		Relieved by 114th Coy. — relief completed 8.30 pm. Moved up from a bivouacs for the night	
	15.10.16		Relieved 113th Coy. in the Left Subsn. Relief complete 7.10 pm. Firing during night 15-16 &	
			Wm — X 2 (C.19 a.2 & 22.36) Target C.7.a.2.2 rounds 1·000	
	16.10.16		Firing during night 16-17th	
			Wm — X 2 Targ. BOLLANEZ (C.7.c.3.5) " 2.0·00	
	17.10.16		Firing during night of 17-18th	
			Wm — X.1. (C.19.a.2.16) Target - Support line rounds 2.1·5·00	
			- X 2 (C.19.a.2.26) - Below do (C.7.c.3.5) 2.1·0·00	
	18.10.16		Firing night 18–19 th	
			Wm X 1. Potizeon Rd. rounds 1·0·00	
			X 2. Bolan Fr. & Potizeon Rd. - 2. 0·00	
			Honeymore during the day	
			Major Bare returned from leave & resumed command	

Army Form C. 2118.

F.S-1

WAR DIARY
or
INTELLIGENCE SUMMARY.
(Erase heading not required.)

Instructions regarding War Diaries and Intelligence Summaries are contained in F. S. Regs., Part II. and the Staff Manual respectively. Title pages will be prepared in manuscript.

Place	Date	Hour	Summary of Events and Information	Remarks and references to Appendices
CANAL BANK	19.10.16		Heavy rain all day. Trenches beginning to flood in places. Liverpool relief carried out. Completed at 9.30 p.m.	
	20.10.16		Fine day – sunny but cold. Repairs to dugouts carried out. No firing was done during night 19/20	LWR
		6 AM	Major Bone left to join Corps School for a month's course	
	21.10.16		Sharp frost – wiring during night 20/21	
			From X1 on Cq A.80.50 to E.8.C.70.30 2000 yds	
		11 AM	F3 Team relieved by team from Reserve in CANAL BANK	
		7 PM	D.1 Team relieved	LWR
	22/10/16		Sharp frost during night – Sunny day	
		10.30 AM	Cq.8 service CANAL BANK	
			Wiring during night 21/22nd	
			From X1 Junction on to Cq.c.4.7 vertical searching to Cq.a.7.2. } 2000 yds
			Cq.d.0.1 Tramway " Cq.a.6.2 }	LWR

T2134. Wt. W703—776. 500000. 4/15. Sir J: C. & S.

Army Form C. 2118.

F 52

WAR DIARY
or
INTELLIGENCE SUMMARY.
(Erase heading not required.)

Place	Date	Hour	Summary of Events and Information	Remarks and references to Appendices
CANAL BK.	23/10/16		Dry Sunny Day. Heavy shelling. Trench mortars re around D1 + D3. Firing carried out during night 22/23rd as follows:—	
			Time — Gun Position — Target — Rds. fired	
		6 P.M. TO 11 P.M.	X.1 — C8d.A.0.50 to C8.c.40.70 — 2000 rds	
			X.2 — C.9.c.60.35 to C.9.c.20.55 — 2000 rds	
			O.1 — CrossRds at C.2.c.80.30 — 1250 rds	
			O.2 — Junctn Trenches at C.2.c.1.65 — 1000	
		11 A.M.	Relief of F.1. F.2 + F.3 commenced — Three Teams leaving from Reserve Canal Bank — Mr Davis relieved Mr Yardley in left subsector.	
		1.45 P.M.	2 Teams of No. 1 Sector relieved Teams at D3 + Y.1. These when relieved, relieved Teams at X.1 + X.2.	
		5 P.M.	Relief of Teams at D1 + N1 carried out — Mr Sowton relieves Mr Godding + takes charge of Right subsector Y1, D1, D3, N1.	[illegible initials]

Army Form C. 2118.

F 53

WAR DIARY
or
INTELLIGENCE SUMMARY.
(Erase heading not required.)

Place	Date	Hour	Summary of Events and Information	Remarks and references to Appendices
CANAL BANK	24/9/16		Bright day. Heavy rain all day. Hung during night 23/24.	
			Position Target Rds.	
			O.1 Pilckem & CANCER TRENCH 2000	
			O.2 C.15.a Central 2000	
			(Gun fired from emplace. C.13.e.3⁴.9	
			X.1 C.8.d.8.3 to C.9.a.1.3 1500	
			X.2 C.2.c.7.4. to C.2.c.9.4. 1500	
			TOTAL 7000	
	25/9/16	7 PM	All guns & kit of 113 M.G. Coy with 2 N.C.O. & 7 men came to CANAL BANK with a view to Relief on night 25/9/16. Bright day but no rain until m.n. Hung during night of 24/25	Lift
			Target – C.2.d.5.2 to C.2.d.9.2 1500 Ms	
			X.1	
			X.2 C.9.c.05 to C.9.c.65 1500 rds	

Army Form C. 2118.

F 54

WAR DIARY
or
INTELLIGENCE SUMMARY.
(Erase heading not required.)

Place	Date	Hour	Summary of Events and Information	Remarks and references to Appendices
CANAL BK.	25/10/16		firing during night 24/25 contd.	
			Bosr O.I.	
			" O.2. C.1.d.0.4 to C.1.d.1.4 1250 rds	
			Target C.14.d.9.6 to C.15.a.1.1 2000 rds	
			(firing at C.13.c.2.4.9)	
			Relief by 113 M.G.C. commenced at 7.30 P.M.	
			" completed successfully by 11.30 P.M.	MR
CAMP S	26/10/16	1.30 AM	All Coy. at Camp 'S'	
			firing during night – Nil. Raining sharply all day.	
A.22.d.8.6.		10 AM	Checking & cleaning of Stores & equipment – fatigue on newhouse standing.	
			2nd Lt. A. Davis proceeded to U.K. on leave.	
	27/10/16	6.45 AM	Reveille – Parades under Section Officers – Cold frosty day.	
		9.30 AM	2nd Lt W. Mailes with a half limber & a runner left for Sheronomes to draw 3 new limbered waggons & conduct same to 113 M.S.C. 114 M.S.C. & 115 M.S.C.	
		1.30 P.M.	1 N.C.O & 10 men to BRIELEN for Rations	

Army Form C. 2118.

F.55

WAR DIARY
or
INTELLIGENCE SUMMARY.
(Erase heading not required.)

Instructions regarding War Diaries and Intelligence Summaries are contained in F. S. Regs., Part II. and the Staff Manual respectively. Title pages will be prepared in manuscript.

Place	Date	Hour	Summary of Events and Information	Remarks and references to Appendices
Camp S.	27/10/16	3 P.M.	Lt G.T HALE & 60 O.R's left to entrain at VESEL HOEK for conveyance to YPRES for cable burying. Heavy rain	
	28/10/16	1.30 A.M.	Cable burying party returned. Cold dull day.	
		8.30 AM	Training under Section officers	
		12.30 PM		
		1.30 PM	5 S.OR's on Horse standing Fatigues.	
		5 PM		
	29/10/16		Cold wet day	
		11. A.M	Left Service - Church army Hut	
		11.30	Non Conformist Service 129 F.A.	
			All the company paraded & change of clothing at Camp E. Wet & very muddy all day.	
	30/10/16	8.30-12	Training under Section officers. Specimen Gun team with all equipment TC laid out for measurement	

T2134. Wt. W708—776. 500000. 4/15. Sir J. C. & S.

Army Form C. 2118.

F 56

WAR DIARY
or
INTELLIGENCE SUMMARY.
(Erase heading not required.)

Instructions regarding War Diaries and Intelligence Summaries are contained in F. S. Regs., Part II. and the Staff Manual respectively. Title pages will be prepared in manuscript.

Place	Date	Hour	Summary of Events and Information	Remarks and references to Appendices
Camp "S"	30/10/16		O.C. To accommodation required for a Veteran Sun Portrait Gymkhana – Col. Pryce – G.S.O.1 38 Div. visited for the demonstration. Took the necessary particulars.	
		1.30–5.30	Horse standing fatigues on our own Horse lines.	
		3 P.M.	2/Lt Southon & 40 O.R's left to entrain at PESELHOEK for Cable burying at CANAL BANK	
			2nd Lt. MAILER returned with limbers from THÉROUANNES.	
			One hundred G.S. wagon with two L.D. Horses added to Transport. Visit from Officer in charge of burying into the feeding of horses in the Corps. Advised closed in ovens &c.	
	31/10/16		Stormy Day – highwinds showery Training under Section Officers.	

W. Morris Lt
Oct 31/16

Army Form C. 2118.

WAR DIARY
or
INTELLIGENCE SUMMARY.
(Erase heading not required.)

Confidential

115 M.G. Coy.

November 1st to 30th. 1916

Vol 7

Army Form C. 2118.

115 M Gun Co

4. 57

WAR DIARY
or
INTELLIGENCE SUMMARY.
(Erase heading not required.)

Instructions regarding War Diaries and Intelligence Summaries are contained in F. S. Regs., Part II. and the Staff Manual respectively. Title pages will be prepared in manuscript.

Place	Date	Hour	Summary of Events and Information	Remarks and references to Appendices
S Camp	1/4/16	8.30	Training under Section officers	
		12 AM		
		1-30-5	Fatigues on Horse standing	
		3 PM	1 Off + 40 O.Rs Carthaging on CANAL BANK.	
	2/4/16	8.30	Training under Section officers	MR
		12 AM		
		10 AM	Lecture on Range Cards to NCOs by Lt Beighley. Brig. Gen. Marden (Temp. Divl. Genl.) paid a spoke about Gun positions what was expected of a Gun Team. No 1 & 2 Section officers late. He inspected the Camp	
		2.27 PM	Wire "Test Alarm" came from 115 Bde	
		2.55 PM	Replied to 115 Bde "Coy not fighting limbers ready to move off" MR	
	3/4/16		Sectional Training	
		11 AM	Paid Company	
		11 AM	Visit from Brig. General Ickles Comndg 115 Bde.	
		1-30-5	Horse standing fatigues	
		4.30 PM	12 Guns 1 NCO & 3 men to M.S. train prior to relief of	

T2134. Wt. W708-776. 500000. 4/15. Sir J. C. & S.

WAR DIARY
or
INTELLIGENCE SUMMARY.
(Erase heading not required.)

Army Form C. 2118.

4. 58

Place	Date	Hour	Summary of Events and Information	Remarks and references to Appendices
'S'camp	3/4/16			
	4/4/16	11am	114 Inf C. went sector	
			2/Lt Evans joined 114 Inf. C. at M.S. farm (It.S.C.9.9.)	n/s
		3.30pm	Teams for huts left for CANAL BK under 2/Lt Yeardley	
		2pm	Officers on line met guides at CANAL BK. Took over in daylight where possible	
		4.30pm	Remainder of Coy with Transport left 'S' Camp	
			4 guns direct to CANAL Bank	
		9 "	Took from M.S. farm to CANAL BANK	W.F.
		6.15pm	Relief commenced	
		9 pm	completed — WIND DANGEROUS	
			Guns disposed as follows:—	
M.S.farm			WILSONS FARM N. } H.Q. THREADNEEDLE ST	
H.Se.9.9			" " E. } No.1 Sector 2/Lt Mailer	
			HILL TOP }	
			VIEW FARM }	
			ENGLISH FARM } H.Q. THREADNEEDLE ST	
			X.9 }	
			THREADNEEDLE ST. } No. 4 Sect. Lt. Hmlo	
			B.13 }	

Army Form C. 2118.

59

WAR DIARY
or
INTELLIGENCE SUMMARY.
(Erase heading not required.)

Place	Date	Hour	Summary of Events and Information	Remarks and references to Appendices
M.G. Farm	4/4/16		FOCH FARM. 2 35 guns in Reserve at M.G. Farm. No 2 Sectn 2/5 Battn of Southn.	
"			KNARESBORO' CASTLE CLIFFORD'S TOWERS LONE WILLOW B.16 No 3 Sectn 2/4th Yorks.	WR
"	5/4/16	9 AM	Lt Bagley interviews G.O.C. at Bde office - visited Lt Subsector.	
		12 noon	During morning night 4/5th mild. Connects mile.	WR
"	6/4/16		Wind dropped to slight breeze - dry & chilly during night 5/6th mild.	
		1 AM	Heavy Bombardment Rt of our trenches on Artillery 12.30 PM - 1 AM Canklekeen.	WR
"		11 AM	Bursts of Shrapnel over VIEW FARM HILLTOP 280 L'POOL ST.	
		2.30 AM	" " ENGLISH FARM.	
		3.15 AM	" " X9 IRISH FARM.	WR

Army Form C. 2118.

4.60

WAR DIARY
or
INTELLIGENCE SUMMARY.
(Erase heading not required.)

Instructions regarding War Diaries and Intelligence Summaries are contained in F. S. Regs., Part II. and the Staff Manual respectively. Title pages will be prepared in manuscript.

Place	Date	Hour	Summary of Events and Information	Remarks and references to Appendices
			Arranged to send Ration parties from M.S. Farm to meet parties from Smithankers Halfway — Right Subsector entrance to THREADNEEDLE ST — Left Subsector — CONEY ST.	
		9 P.M	Our artillery started bombardment S of YPRES & could intermittently hear mm	
	7/11/16	6 AM	firing during the night 6th-7th from 6 PM — 3 AM	
			TARGET	
			Position X 9	e.16, 16.66 to C.16.b.2.7 & 3 Trench &s/men 1500 Ver Sand to CANOE TRENCH THREADNEEDLE ST. C.17.b.5.2. to C.17.8.8.5. 1500 TOTAL 3000	
			Pouring with Rain all day. Cleared about 3 P.M.	
		11 AM	Sent up Number Boards for Sniferpokers 13.13, THREADNEEDLE ST. (CLIFFORD TOWERS, ENGLISH FARM, HILL TOP, WILSON FARM N, WILSON FARM E, LONE WILLOW, FOCH FARM.	
		9.30 PM	Cpl Hardy we Tom Leave to UK 8 – 18 LWS	

T2134. Wt. W708—776. 500000. 4/15. Sir J. C. & S.

Army Form C. 2118.

461.

WAR DIARY
or
INTELLIGENCE SUMMARY.
(Erase heading not required.)

Place	Date	Hour	Summary of Events and Information	Remarks and references to Appendices
	8/4/16		Bright morning.	
			During during night — 2 S.I. from 9 PM – 1 AM.	
			TARGET.	
			Position	Rds
			X 9 — C.9.d.8.0 TO C10.c.1.5 ½ KALENDAR AVENUE	1000
				1000
			THREADNEEDLE ST. C24.c.6.3 TO C24.C.4.6	
			TOTAL = 2000	
		11 AM.	During today bursts of shrapnel were reported at CLIFFORD TOWERS, TURCO FARM, LIVERPOOL ST. near VIEW FARM & HILLTOP	
		2 PM	Several Whizzbangs in front of B.13. During the day towards trench repair was carried at most positions heavy rains having greatly added to take place in trenches. C.R.A. corps visited ENGLISH FARM – under consideration as an O.P.	
		5 PM.	Interteam relief carried out. 2nd Lt Santhon relieved 2nd Lt Godding.	LWR

T2134. Wt. W708–776. 500000. 4/15. Sir J. C. & S.

Army Form C. 2118.

462

WAR DIARY
or
INTELLIGENCE SUMMARY.
(Erase heading not required.)

Instructions regarding War Diaries and Intelligence Summaries are contained in F. S. Regs., Part II. and the Staff Manual respectively. Title pages will be prepared in manuscript.

Place	Date	Hour	Summary of Events and Information	Remarks and references to Appendices
		6 PM	2nd Lt DAVIS returned from leave to UK.	
	9/1/16	9.30 PM	2nd Lts. Godding & Davis on Bivouac & M.G. Scheme. Enemy shining night 8 P - 9 P.	
			<table><tr><th>Position</th><th>Target</th><th>Time</th><th>Rounds</th></tr><tr><td>X 9 fired from C 27. a. 6. 5.</td><td>E 9. d. 8. 0 to C 10. C. 1. S. Vert. search along Rd & Rly Track & CALENDAR AVENUE</td><td>5.45 PM + 12 mn</td><td>1000</td></tr><tr><td>THREAD NEEDLE St fired from C 27. d. 12. 42.</td><td>C 24. c. 6. 4. To C 24. c. 3. 5 Traverse. along CAMBRAI Drive, Rly TRACK & PLUM FARM</td><td>5.15 PM TO 1 AM</td><td>1000</td></tr></table>	
		8.30 AM	Enemy shelling towards BRIE 16 N - several such Planes about during morning & anti aircraft busy	MR

T2134. Wt. W708-776. 500000. 4/15. Sir J. C. & S.

WAR DIARY
or
INTELLIGENCE SUMMARY.
(Erase heading not required.)

Army Form C. 2118.

463

Place	Date	Hour	Summary of Events and Information	Remarks and references to Appendices
	10/11/16		Firing during night 9th – 10th	

Position	TARGET	Time	Rds
X.9. hung from c 29.a.65	OBLONG FARM & Rly/tracks C.16.b.6.1½ TO C16.b.4.3 Traversing	5 PM TO 6 PM & 12 to 3 am	1000 rds
THREADNEEDLE ST.	CAMBRAI AVENUE & Rly/tracks C 23.d.3.9 TO C 23.d.5.7	5 PM – 6 PM & 12 to 3 AM	1000

| | | 10 PM | Cpl Walmsley & 1 left AA Browulee to Bde for instruction in observation. Fair aerial & artillery activity during the day | WR |
| | 11/11/16 | 7 PM | Lt. W.T. Bongley went to 1st Dg. D.A. Schutten. Firing during night 10th – 11th | WR |

Position	TARGET	Time	Rds
THREADNEEDLE ST	CAMBRAI AVENUE & Rly tracks C23.d.3.9 To C23.d.5.7	5·30 PM – 12·30 AM	1000
X.9	OBLONG FARM & Rly Tracks C16.b.6.1½ To C16.b.4.3	5·30 PM – 12·30 AM	1000

Army Form C. 2118.

WAR DIARY
or
INTELLIGENCE SUMMARY.
(Erase heading not required.)

Instructions regarding War Diaries and Intelligence Summaries are contained in F. S. Regs., Part II. and the Staff Manual respectively. Title pages will be prepared in manuscript.

7.6.4

Place	Date	Hour	Summary of Events and Information	Remarks and references to Appendices
	11/4/16		Enemy busy during day with shrapnel wiring, barrage work & overhauling of stores at gun positions	MR
	12/4/16		Dry morning – ground becoming firmer. Dry during night 11/12th	
			<table> <tr><th>Position</th><th>Target</th><th>Time</th><th>Rds</th></tr> <tr><td>THREADNEEDLE ST.</td><td>Crossrds. & Trolley lines in front of Von Hugel Farm C23.c.7½.7 – C23.d.1.4½</td><td>6.30 PM TO 12 mn</td><td>1000</td></tr> <tr><td>X.9</td><td>CARAMEL TRACKS & Rly lines C16.b.4.8 TO C16.b.7.5.</td><td>6.30 PM TO 12 mn</td><td>1000</td></tr> </table>	
		6AM	"A" frame Trench boards breastwork frames sent to KNARESBORO' CASTLE & X.9. Artillery on both sides active during day. Air quiet	MR

Army Form C. 2118.

WAR DIARY
or
INTELLIGENCE SUMMARY.
(Erase heading not required.)

Instructions regarding War Diaries and Intelligence Summaries are contained in F. S. Regs., Part II. and the Staff Manual respectively. Title pages will be prepared in manuscript.

765

Place	Date	Hour	Summary of Events and Information	Remarks and references to Appendices
M.G. Farm	13/11/16		Bright dry day — misty in afternoon. Firing during night 12-13th	
			<table><tr><td>Position</td><td>Target</td><td>Time</td><td>Rds</td></tr><tr><td>THREADNEEDLE ST.</td><td>CARNATION TRENCH trolley lines C23.b.8k.4. TO C23.d.9.9 traversing</td><td>6 P.M to 12 mn</td><td>1000</td></tr><tr><td>X 9.</td><td>Trenches, Trolley lines rune in front KITCHENER'S WOOD C.16.b.7.9 TO C.17.a.2.6½ traversing</td><td>6 P.M TO 12 mn</td><td>1000</td></tr></table>	
			Enemy artillery fairly busy during the day. Enemy plane over CANAL BANK 3.30 P.M drove back	Kitchener

Army Form C. 2118.

WAR DIARY
or
INTELLIGENCE SUMMARY.
(Erase heading not required.)

Place	Date	Hour	Summary of Events and Information	Remarks and references to Appendices
M.G. Farm	14/11/16		Firing during night 13th–14th as follows:—	

Position	TARGET	Time	Rds
THREADNEEDLE ST.	Trolley line, Tracks & Trenches near BRIDGE HOUSE C.14.a.2.10 TO C.14.a.6.2	7 PM TO 12 mn	1000
X 9	CARAMEL TRENCH & Trolley line Tracks C.16.6.7.9. TO C.17.a.2.6	7 PM TO 12 mn	1000

2 PM Relief by 114 M.G. Coy commenced. The following guns were relieved in daytime CLIFFORD TOWERS, KNARESBORO' CASTLE, THREADNEEDLE ST., X 9.

3.30 AM Teams for relief of guns moved off from CANAL BANK — the following were relieved at dusk:— LONE WILLOW, WILSON FARM N.E, ENGLISH FARM HILLTOP FARM, VIEW FARM, B.16, FOCH FARM B.13.

5.30 PM Stores & personnel in Reserve moved to BURGOMASTER FARM —

6.30 PM Relief complete.

Army Form C. 2118.

WAR DIARY
or
INTELLIGENCE SUMMARY.
(Erase heading not required.)

Instructions regarding War Diaries and Intelligence Summaries are contained in F. S. Regs., Part II. and the Staff Manual respectively. Title pages will be prepared in manuscript.

467

Place	Date	Hour	Summary of Events and Information	Remarks and references to Appendices
BURGOMASTER FARM	15th Nov.	12 noon	Relief of 113 M.G. Coy commenced — nine guns relieved by day. Officers & N.C.O's took over in daytime. Positions relieved by day F.1 (C13.b.1.4), P.1 (C13.a.3.7) O.3 (C13.a.5½.4) Y.1 (C19.b.2.8) D.3 (C14.c.2.4) O.1 (C13.a.3½.2) O.2 (C13.a.3½.3) X.1 (C19.a.1½.7) X.2 (C19.a.2.3)	
		3.15 P.M	Team for night relief moved off from BURGOMASTER F.M. The following relief was carried out at dusk :- D.1 (C14.c.9.1) N.1 (C20.a.2.4) P.4 (?) (C12.a.7½.8) Z.1 (C12.c.4.5).	
		6.15 P.M	Relief complete. Casualties nil.	WR
	16th Nov		Firing during night 15th - 16th nil	
		6 A.M.	Guns from D.1 & D.3 withdrawn owing to our bombardment near CAESAR'S NOSE & HIGH COMMAND REDOUBT	
		4.30 P.M.	Guns retd. to D.1 & D.3. Preparation of emplacements for night firing at O.1. & T.1. x 2. Casualties nil.	WR

Army Form C. 2118.

WAR DIARY
or
INTELLIGENCE SUMMARY.
(Erase heading not required.)

4 - 68

Place	Date	Hour	Summary of Events and Information	Remarks and references to Appendices
CANAL BANK	17/11/16	6AM	Guns from R1 & D.3 withdrawn.	
		9.30AM	Lieut S.T Hale left to go on leave U.K. 18th Nov - 28th Nov	
		4PM	Cpl D.J Brown 11917 reported at 'P'Corps Trench Mortar Training Coy. for VIII Corps School.	
		4.30PM	Guns ret'd to R1 & D.3	
		11PM	Firing from 5 guns to assist raid by 14th R.W.F. on HIGH COMMAND REDOUBT.	
		11.35PM		

Position		Target	Time	Rds
Emplacements on CANAL B.K from X1 x 2 & Reserve Line	(a) Area enclosed by C8.d.9.2.0, C8.d.8.2.2, C9.c.5.3.3½, + C9.c.4.5		11PM	3000
	(b) " " C14.b.8.4.6, C14.b.7½.7, C15.a.3½.9½, + C15.a.3.7.8		11.35	
	(c) " " C9.c.½.2 to C9.c.5.4			
Guns from O2 in straight position	Area enclosed by C9.c.5.0, C15.a.6.½, C15.a.9½.7½, + C9.c.7.4.1		11.15 / 11.35	850

Army Form C. 2118.

WAR DIARY
or
INTELLIGENCE SUMMARY.
(Erase heading not required.)

Place	Date	Hour	Summary of Events and Information	Remarks and references to Appendices
CANAL BK.	17/1/16	11 PM TO 11.35	Army was also carried from N.1 on area Cgc.75.3z, Cgc.10.z, Cg.d.z.9z, Cg.d.4z.7 Rd. river 1150. — Sharp frost Casualties nil	
	18/1/16		Very cold weather	nil
		8.30 AM	2/Lt Mailer went to Corps H.Q. to demonstration on the Armstrong Packs.	
			Filling of Belts — cleaning of trench boards &c	
		2.30 AM	Gas alarm — false alarm due to aeroplane passing over.	
			Sharp frost during night	
	19/1/16	9 AM	2/Lt Souttar left to attend inspection by the Corps Commander of Ravine party to on the 11 Command Redoubt — Completed M.Gunner Sergt Newell M/G Dept/M attended also	W.R.
		11.45	Church Service CANAL BK	
		4 PM	Major Bove returns from Corps School & resumed command Inter Team Relief took place	

Army Form C. 2118.

WAR DIARY
or
INTELLIGENCE SUMMARY.
(Erase heading not required.)

Instructions regarding War Diaries and Intelligence Summaries are contained in F. S. Regs., Part II. and the Staff Manual respectively. Title pages will be prepared in manuscript.

4 7 0

Place	Date	Hour	Summary of Events and Information	Remarks and references to Appendices
CANAL BK.		noon	Wind safe	
			hvy hvy nght 18th-19th	
			from C.19.a.2.8 (CACTUS BK.) - Traversing fire from MACKENSEN FARM (C8c)	
			To CACTUS OT (C7b.) 1250 rds	
			Casualties nil	
	20th Nov		Nothing during night 19th-20th	
			Dull day & cold wind - wind safe	MWR
	21st		Firing during the night 7th-8th	
			Firing during night 20-21st	
	22nd		from area N.I. target:- C.2.c.4.2.2 to C.2.c.8.4.0 - Rds fired 200	hvy
			firing during night 21st-22nd	
			Concentrated fire on HINDENBURG FARM 6-6.30 PM. Retaliation	
			immediately with 1½" shrapnel & H.E.	
			Target 6.30 - 12 mm (a) C.9.a.5.3½ to C.9.a.9.4.	
			(b) C.15.d. 20.90 to C.15.d. 50.00	
			Total Rds fired = 5200	
		5 PM	Lt. W. T. Bougher returned from hospital	
	23	3 PM	~~~~~~~~~~~~~~ 2/Lt Ambrose returned to Corps Officers School	reported
		10 AM	Lt Col HARP U.A. Corp M.S. Officer visited the Coy	MWR

T2134. Wt. W708—776. 500000. 4/15. Sir J. C. & S.

Army Form C. 2118.

WAR DIARY
or
INTELLIGENCE SUMMARY.
(Erase heading not required.)

Place	Date	Hour	Summary of Events and Information	Remarks and references to Appendices
CANAL BANK	Mar 23rd		Firing during night 22/23.	4/71

Location	Targets	Rds.
X1	C.9.c.3.3 – C.9.d.1.2 Tramways leading to Below Fm. & Hindenburg Fm.	2000
X2	C.2.d.5t.1t – C.2.d.10.0 Tramways Rtn. near CANDLE AVENUE	2000
C.13.c.3t.9t	C.15.a.7.8 to C.15.b.10.3. Below Fm. to Müller Cot.	1500
	TOTAL	5500 Rds

MR

Inter Team relief carried out.
Artillery activity on both sides
strong during night of 23/24.

Lt B.

Army Form C. 2118.

WAR DIARY
or
INTELLIGENCE SUMMARY.
(Erase heading not required.)

Instructions regarding War Diaries and Intelligence Summaries are contained in F. S. Regs., Part II. and the Staff Manual respectively. Title pages will be prepared in manuscript.

Page 2

Place	Date	Hour	Summary of Events and Information	Remarks and references to Appendices
CANAL BANK				
				1ST B
			Position / Target	
			X1 Y 2 / CAESAR'S AVENUE	
			/ indirect searching from 2300ˣ to 2500ˣ 3,000 Rds	
			C.13.a.35.10 / C.9.d.28.95. 1,000	
			P.1 / C.9.C.55.05. 1,000	
24	24/25		X1 Y 2 Occasional bursts during the night on C.9.d.50.05., Headcorn Farm, C.8.d.95.20. and vital search Caesar Avenue 20 rounds fired 3,000.	1ST B
25		6 pm	Relieved in the Left Sector by 113th M.G. Coy. Relief completed 9.40 pm. Marched to Camp "S" & took over billets vacated by 113 d Coy. 2/Lt. L.W. Evans, 2/Lt. R.M. Dawson & 2/Lt. T. Lundey (date not known (?))	KTB

Lieutenant

Army Form C. 2118.

WAR DIARY
or
INTELLIGENCE SUMMARY.
(Erase heading not required.)

Place	Date	Hour	Summary of Events and Information	Remarks and references to Appendices
CAMP "S"	25th		Lt Yardley & 4 O.Rs returned from M.G. School at CAMIERS	AS.
	26th	11am	Church Parade for 2 O/ & 80 O.Rs remainder	LT P.S.
			Haircutting & issue of Razors	
	27th		Cleaning of stores & under packing	
		2PM	Company Padout	
		4PM	2 Officers & 110 O.Rs Cable Burying near CANAL BANK	
		12PM	Party returned from CANAL B.K.	KMR
		9PM	Gas alarm - 1 hour	
	28th	7AM	50 men to Baths — 2/Lt D.P. Pollock reported for duty.	
		8AM	50 men to Baths	KMR
			Training under Sector officers	
	29th		Company training under Sector officers	
			Horse standing fatigues 1 c 50 O.Rs	
		4.55PM	"TEST ALARM" Coy turned out	
		5.30PM	Coy ready to move	

Army Form C. 2118.

WAR DIARY
or
INTELLIGENCE SUMMARY.
(Erase heading not required.)

Place	Date	Hour	Summary of Events and Information	Remarks and references to Appendices
Camp	29th	5.12	Transport ready to move	
		5.17PM		
		7PM	Coy Concert in Church Army Hut	
	30th		Intague to Bri. School & Horse Standings — Pitching of equipment	Kulvar
		2.30AM	Brigade Inspection by Corps Commander at E Camp. Presentation of medals for & meritorious conduct in raid on HIGH COMMAND REDOUBT 17th Nov.	Kulvar

Army Form C. 2118.

WAR DIARY
or
INTELLIGENCE SUMMARY.
(Erase heading not required.)

Vol 8

Summary of Events and Information

CONFIDENTIAL

115 Machine Gun Company

December 1st
To
December 31st 1916

Army Form C. 2118.

F75

WAR DIARY
or
INTELLIGENCE SUMMARY.
(Erase heading not required.)

Instructions regarding War Diaries and Intelligence Summaries are contained in F. S. Regs., Part II. and the Staff Manual respectively. Title pages will be prepared in manuscript.

Place	Date	Hour	Summary of Events and Information	Remarks and references to Appendices
S Camp A 23.6.48	1/1/16	9 AM	Training section officers w.o.	
		1 PM	Police practice carried out	
	2/1/16	10 AM	Inspection of Camp & Training by Brig-Gen Hickie.	Wst
		10 AM	Firing on Range Part 1 Table 'C' Practice 1, 2 & 3	Wst
	3/1/16	3 PM		
		11 AM	Church Parades C. of E. 11 AM.	
		11.30 AM	Nonconformist Parade	
		3.30 PM	13 guns 1 officer 1 Sergt 45 men to Canal Bk. Rt Sector prior to relief of 114 M.G.C.	Wst
	4/1/16	10 AM	4 officers left for Canal Bk. To take over gun positions	
		12 noon	Teams for line left for Canal Bk.	
		3.30 PM	Remainder of company left S'Camp	
CANAL BK Cag.c.1.6		6 PM	Relief of 114 M.G. Coy completed the following positions were occupied	
			C 22.1 B13	
			C 27.2 THREADNEEDLE ST.	

WAR DIARY
or
INTELLIGENCE SUMMARY.

Army Form C. 2118.

F.76

Place	Date	Hour	Summary of Events and Information	Remarks and references to Appendices
			X.9 C.22.c.1.2	
			C.27.3 ENGLISH FM. C.27.b.5½.3	
			C.21.4. HILLTOP FM. C.21.d.1½.9	
			— VIEW FM. C.21.c.8½.8	
			C.26.1 WILSONS FM N. C.26.b.4½.1½	
			C.26.2 WILSONS FM. E. C.26.d.6.9½	
			— B.16 C.21.a.9.8	
			C.20.2 LONEWILLOW C.20.b.6.5.	
			— KNARESBORO C.20.b.8.9½	
			— CASTLE	
			C.21.1 CLIFFORD C.21.a.3½.8½	
			TOWERS	
			— FOCH FM. C.20.d.2.9½	
			Coy. H.Q. C.19. c.2½.6.	
Camp	8/9/19		nothing during night 4/5th.	mR
			very not quiet during night 4/5th.	

Army Form C. 2118.

F.77

WAR DIARY
or
INTELLIGENCE SUMMARY.
(Erase heading not required.)

Instructions regarding War Diaries and Intelligence Summaries are contained in F. S. Regs., Part II. and the Staff Manual respectively. Title pages will be prepared in manuscript.

Place	Date	Hour	Summary of Events and Information	Remarks and references to Appendices
	5/9/16		Casualties to known nil. Wind Dangerous.	
	6/9/16		Bryant commenced at X.9 THREADNEEDLE ST firing during night 5/6.	MG
			Position — Stirling Lane 13 (night position) Casualties nil.	Rds 1750
	7/9/16		Very misty - all day. Enemy shelling about 7 - 7.30 AM. Bryant at KNARESBORO CASTLE heavy/sharp bang - slight damage. firing during night 6-7. In between 6 - 11 PM.	MG
			Target	Rds
			Northern STIRLING LANE PICKEM VILLAGE	2000
			THREADNEEDLE ST Cqd.10.05 to Cqd.80.95 Junct. of Rds & Rly Trenches	2000

WAR DIARY
or
INTELLIGENCE SUMMARY.
(Erase heading not required.)

Army Form C. 2118.

F78

Place	Date	Hour	Summary of Events and Information	Remarks and references to Appendices
	8/7/16	3.30 AM	In front of parapet on both fronts reconnaissance of ground opposite line.	
		8 PM	Bombardment in enemy lines. 2 officers 116 MG Coy visited sector with a view to preliminary reconnaissance.	MWR
	9/7/16		Misty — slight rain during day + night. 7-8 PM 7-11 PM	

Position	Target	
STIRLING LANE 15	C8.b.7.8k to C8.b.10.8½ & C8.b.6.4½	2000
	To C8.b.9.4	
THREADNEEDLE ST.	Cg.c.1.4. to Cg.c.5.4 Comms Tracks & Communic Trenches	2000.

| | | 5 PM | 2 coms at HILLTOP, B13, B16, KNARESBORO CASTLE, ECCH FM, CLIFFOR TOWERS, LONEWILLOW relieved | |
| | | 11 AM | 2 officers from 116 bridge visited sector for preliminary reconnaissance | MWR. |

Army Form C. 2118.

F 79

WAR DIARY
or
INTELLIGENCE SUMMARY.
(Erase heading not required.)

Instructions regarding War Diaries and Intelligence Summaries are contained in F. S. Regs., Part II. and the Staff Manual respectively. Title pages will be prepared in manuscript.

Place	Date	Hour	Summary of Events and Information	Remarks and references to Appendices
	9/11/16		Fire during night 8th – 9th	
			Gun position	
			THREADNEEDLE ST.	Rds. fired
			Target	2000
			Junct. Rly. Rds. T Trades	
		6AM	Cg.b.20.05 to Cg.d.80.95	
			fired at C27.d.2.8 & contd until 7.30AM	
			Target :– Cg.b.20.05 – Cg.d.80.95 Rds fired 750	
		7.30AM	Guns laid to meet possible raid on rt. of sector – WIEITJE	M.8.
	10/11/16	10.30AM	R.E. service	
			Enemy active on rt. of sector	
			All 4 guns laid on targets to meet possible raid on	
			WIEITJE area	M.8.
	11/11/16		Arrangements made for relief of 118 M.G. Coy in left sector	
		1.30PM	4 officers from 116 M.G.C. took over at gun positions in Rt. Sector	
		6PM	Relief of 116 M.G.C. commenced	
		9.30PM	" " " completed	
		11.30PM	Last of Coy. left CANAL Bg for "S" Camp	MR

T2134. Wt. W708—776. 500000. 4/15. Sir J. C. & S.

Army Form C. 2118.

F 80

WAR DIARY
or
INTELLIGENCE SUMMARY.
(Erase heading not required.)

Instructions regarding War Diaries and Intelligence Summaries are contained in F.S. Regs., Part II. and the Staff Manual respectively. Title pages will be prepared in manuscript.

Place	Date	Hour	Summary of Events and Information	Remarks and references to Appendices
S'Camp	12/9/16	12.30 AM	Officers & N.C.O's left for H.Q. 118MGC. To be guided to Gunpositions in left Section.	
		2 AM	Teams & H.Q. with hurdles left for DECOUCK F.M.	
		3.45	Teams for positions left X rds ELVERDINGHE. (B.14.b.3.6.)	
DECOUCK F.M.		9.15 PM	Relief of 118 MGC completed the following gunpositions occupied :-	
B.13.6.2.8.			"A" Line A6. B.13.a.95.80.	
			"B" Line. (B1). B.6.c.18.00. (B.2) B.12.a.45.55. (B.3) B.12.a.70.30. (B.4) B.12.d.0595.	
			"C" Line. (C1) B.11.d.90.00. (C3) B.11.d.10.80. (C4) B.11.a.85.15. (C5) B.11.a.75.40.	
			"L" Defences :- SALVATION CORNER. I.1.c.90.80.	
			WAGRAM FARM. B.23 central. Section O/c. H.Q.s	
			REIGERSBERG. H.6.a.60.90. at B.11.6.95.70.	
			WINDMILL. H.6.b.20.40. and B.11.d.45.05. GOW	
	13/9/16	10 am	Nord Opens fired during night 12th/13th. No artillery or M.G. activity on either side. None opens fired during night 13th/14th. "A" + "B" lines were trench mortared by 5pm. evening between 3.30 pm and 5 pm. 20 L.H.V. shto comeover. Retaliation 5pm. Grenallier NK GOW	

Army Form C. 2118.

WAR DIARY
or
INTELLIGENCE SUMMARY.
(Erase heading not required.)

Instructions regarding War Diaries and Intelligence Summaries are contained in F. S. Regs., Part II. and the Staff Manual respectively. Title pages will be prepared in manuscript.

F 81

Place	Date	Hour	Summary of Events and Information	Remarks and references to Appendices
DECOUCK FM.	14/12/16	11 am.	Two Reinforcements arrived from Base. 2/Lt Boughy returned from leave to UK.	
		8.30	Enemy shelled Church & Chateau & railway at BOESINGHE with H.E.	
		9 pm.		
	15/7/16		O.C. & 2/I/C made a reconnaissance of the line with reference to the loops in G Defence Scheme.	
	16/7/16		3 Other Ranks returned from h.q. School Camiers. Our machine guns fired on enemy trench railways — rounds fired 1500	
	17/7/16		2/Lt Coulter returned to duty from hospital. Enemy Ins fell on BOESINGHE WOOD & VILLAGE. Our guns again fired on enemy trench railway — rounds fired 1500. 2/Lt Parker & 3 other ranks to Course of Physical Training & Bayonet fighting.	
	18/7/16		Our guns fired 1500 rounds on enemy trench railways 2/Lt Davis Fitzjohn 7/Lincs dated Aug 1st 1916. No 53331 Sergt Bent appointed C.Q.M.S ft 25 M.G. Coy.	

Army Form C. 2118.

WAR DIARY
or
INTELLIGENCE SUMMARY.
(Erase heading not required.)

F. 82

Instructions regarding War Diaries and Intelligence Summaries are contained in F. S. Regs., Part II., and the Staff Manual respectively. Title pages will be prepared in manuscript.

Place	Date	Hour	Summary of Events and Information	Remarks and references to Appendices
DECOUCK FARM	19/12/16	9 a.m.	Enemy artillery and Trench Mortars active on our Front line and BOESINGHE. Aircraft very active during the day. Three enemy machines flew over our lines.	
	20/12/16		Intermittent Relief carried out during afternoon. Relief complete by 6.30 p.m. We did not fire any guns. Corps Commander altered the name of our Support Reserve lines. Support line to be called "S" line and reserve line the "X" line.	
		12 mid. to 2.30 p.m.	Our Trench mortars and Field Artillery registered on German Front Supportline.	
	21/12/16.		Our guns fired on enemy trench railways. Rounds fired 200. Enemy artillery and trench mortars active all day on our front line and BOESINGHE. Our retaliation better - chiefly with 18 pdrs.	
	22/12/16		One reinforcement arrived. Enemy artillery active during day - especially on Belgium Right flank. We did not fire any guns.	
	23/12/16	2 a.m.	Heavy and intense enemy bombardment in this sector with Trench Mortars, L.H.V. and H.E. shells. Lasted till 3 a.m. Small raiding party entered trenches on our right and held with some prisoners.	
		2 p.m. to 4 p.m.	Heavy bombardment by our trench mortars and artillery of enemy front, support, reserve lines.	

GM.

Army Form C. 2118.

WAR DIARY
or
INTELLIGENCE SUMMARY.
(Erase heading not required.)

F 83

Place	Date	Hour	Summary of Events and Information	Remarks and references to Appendices
DECOUCK FM	23/12/16		Two men wounded during enemy bombardment. We did not fire any guns.	
	24/12/16		Church of England Parade 9.30 am. R.C. 11.30 am. Somewhere. Our aircraft very active during day. Enemy artillery very quiet. Slow bombardment by our guns during the day. We did not fire any guns.	
	25/12/16	9 am	Church of England Parade. ELVERDINGHE.	
		11.30 am	R.C. Parade somewhere.	
	26/12/16		2nd Lieut. Moller and 3 other ranks returned from Physical Training Course.	
	25/12/16		Slow bombardment by our guns and trench mortars and rifle grenades during the	
		3 p.m.	day. Lively enemy retaliation chiefly with trench mortars till 4.30 p.m. We fired	
		6 p.m.	1500 rounds on HODDLESTON ROAD	
		6.30 p.m.	Lieut. Am. Souther granted leave to U.K. 26-12-1916 to 5-1-1917.	
	26/12/16		Intermittent shelling during the day. We did not fire any guns.	
		1 p.m.	The O.C. and 2nd in Command with 2 other ranks proceed to VIII Corps School.	
			One N.C.O. sent to Divisional Gas School.	
		2 p.m.	Lieut. L.W. Evans returned from leave to U.K.	
		6 p.m.	2nd Lieut. L.F. Brown joined company as reinforcement from CAMIERS. 2nd Lieut. A.C. Golding appointed to command the Coy. during the O.C. & 2nd in Com's absence. O.T.A.	

Army Form C. 2118.

WAR DIARY
or
INTELLIGENCE SUMMARY.
(Erase heading not required.)

F. 84

Instructions regarding War Diaries and Intelligence Summaries are contained in F.S. Regs., Part II. and the Staff Manual respectively. Title pages will be prepared in manuscript.

Place	Date	Hour	Summary of Events and Information	Remarks and references to Appendices
DE COUDEKERQUE	27/12/16		Artillery quieter on both sides.	
		9 am	Lieut L.W. Evans leaves the Coy, on being appointed 2i/c in Command of 116 M.G. Coy. 2 international Relief carried out.	
	28/12/16	1 pm	3 O.R. reinforcements from CAMIERS arrived. Artillery on both sides fairly active all day.	
	29/12/16		Air fired on enemy trench railways with one gun. Rds expended 1,000.	
	30/12/16	9 pm	Relieved in the line by the 116 & M.G. Coy. Relief complete 9pm.	
		10.30 pm	M.G., O. & 2nd in Command + 3 O.R. returned from Bn Camp Creek.	
		8 pm	Company paraded & marched to CHEESE MARKET STATION - POPERINGHE entrained & proceeded to BOLLEZEELE.	
BOLLEZEELE	31/12/16	2.30 am	Arrived at BOLLEZEELE and proceeded to billets.	
		6 pm	Day spent in cleaning up. C.F.E. Sevrin M.S. resting in billets.	

J.F. Bow Major 15 C.C.
Comdt 15 M.G.C.

Army Form C. 2118.

WAR DIARY
or
INTELLIGENCE SUMMARY.
(Erase heading not required.)

Summary of Events and Information

Confidential

115 M.G. Co.

Jan 1st to Jan 31st 1917

Vol 9

Army Form C. 2118.

WAR DIARY
or
INTELLIGENCE SUMMARY.
(Erase heading not required.)

F. S.

Instructions regarding War Diaries and Intelligence Summaries are contained in F.S. Regs., Part II. and the Staff Manual respectively. Title pages will be prepared in manuscript.

Place	Date	Hour	Summary of Events and Information	Remarks and references to Appendices
BOLLEZEELE	1.1.17	7.45 am	Morning Cleaning Parade	
		8.45	Cos Training – General Cleaning at & guns & etc	
		– 1/pm	after bm of trench duty	
	2.1.17	8.45 am to 1 pm	Company Training	
	3.1.17	"	"	
	4.1.17	"	2/2 Duffork admitted to hospital Route march with "Action" from livens (advanced training)	
	5.1.17	"	Advanced Gun Drill in Enemy area followed by Tactical Scheme – Enemy firing exercises in village fighting Lt. Hale & 4 O.R's admitted to hospital.	
	6.1.17	8.45 am to 1 pm	Company Training under Coln Officer	
	7.1.17	9 am	Church Parade for Presbyterian	
		10.15 am	" C. of E.	
		11.30 am	" R. C.	N.B.
		2.30 pm	Company Lothrax tour played Brigade H.Q. team in Brigade Cup Final Score Bn H.Q. 2 M.G.C. 1	
	8.1.17	8.45 am	Company paraded for tactical exercise extract	

Army Form C. 2118.

WAR DIARY
or
INTELLIGENCE SUMMARY.
(Erase heading not required.)

F-86

Instructions regarding War Diaries and Intelligence Summaries are contained in F. S. Regs., Part II. and the Staff Manual respectively. Title pages will be prepared in manuscript.

Place	Date	Hour	Summary of Events and Information	Remarks and references to Appendices
Bollezeele	8.1.17		included practice in Wood fighting	
		4 pm	Brigade Boxing Tournament. Company Carpenter took 13th place & of the Company team won through to the semi-final.	
	9.1.17	9 am	No. 15355 P.G. W. Leeman tried by F.G.C.M. The Court assembled at Coy H.Q.	
		2.30 pm	Cross Country Run. Company team finished 3rd	
		4 pm	Brigade Final. Bde. W.O. & M.G. Coy (Coy. leader by 10 Cos. W.B.	
	10.1.17		Range Practice under Section Officers. 1 Off. & 2 O.R.s parted leave to UK.	
	11.1.17		Parades cancelled on account of inclement weather	
	12.1.17	8.45 pm	Company participated in Brigade attack scheme	
	13.1.17	3.15 pm	Company Training.	
"E" CAMP.	14.1.17	9 am	Company entrained for POPERINGHE	
		2 pm	Arrived at POPERINGHE and marched to "E" Camp	
	15.1.17	8 pm	1 Officer & 3 O.R.s proceeded to M.G. School, CAMIERS.	W.T.B.
		2 pm	Company moved to "S" Camp	

Army Form C. 2118.

E-87

WAR DIARY
or
INTELLIGENCE SUMMARY.
(Erase heading not required.)

Place	Date	Hour	Summary of Events and Information	Remarks and references to Appendices
"S" Camp	15.1.17	2 pm	1 Off. & 20 O.R. proceeded on leave to U.K.	
Luches	16.1.17	3.30 pm	Company relieved 116 Lt Coy in the BOESINGHE SECTOR	
		7.45pm	Relief Complete.	
			Disposition - 3 guns in front line, 4 in Support & 4 in Reserve and 6 at Company H.Q.	
	17.1.17	9.30am	Took over position at SALVATION CORNER temporarily.	
			Very quiet in the line.	
		4pm	Position at SALVATION CORNER taken over by 117 Lt Coy	
	18.1.17	9am	Enemy's artillery active on Support line damaging trench near gun positions. No casualties. Machine gun quiet.	
	19.1.17	2pm	Major Bone & 20 O.R proceeded on leave to U.K. Lieut. Boughey assumed temporary command of the Company	
		2.30pm	2 guns in front line withdrawn by order of Brig General 68 as it is considered that the very small field of fire obtainable does not justify the employment of Vickers Guns. Position taken over by Lewis guns of the Battalion in the line.	

1570

Army Form C. 2118.

WAR DIARY
or
INTELLIGENCE SUMMARY.
(Erase heading not required.)

F.88

Instructions regarding War Diaries and Intelligence Summaries are contained in F. S. Regs., Part II and the Staff Manual respectively. Title pages will be prepared in manuscript.

Place	Date	Hour	Summary of Events and Information	Remarks and references to Appendices
Trenches	19.1.17		Enemy Artillery active against our lines today. 15 N.E. shells falling near X.1 position.	
"	20.1.17	11 am	2/Lt Brown proceeded to Divisional School for course of Instruction. Enemy artillery again active neighbourhood of Z.1. Shelled with H.E. and L.H.V. — No casualties. Three 7 cm 12 pdr shells fell short in BOESINGHE or other hanging a dugout at an Section N.0m.	
"	21.1.17		Information received that the actions of 2 guns H.L. found in N°15.35.c Artly 2nd Army Ltr. N°CM 12968 d/18-1-17. Pte W. Ullman to suspended.	
"	22.1.17	1.30 pm 2 pm	6 S.I. shells fell near Z.1. position. No casualties. Interested reliefs carried out. Relief completed. No casualties. Enemy artillery activity maintained. No casualties. Communication between front teams on it's X line suspended – on to jumper in slow on account of the hard frost.	
"		11 am	2/Lts Golding & 2.O.R's returned from leave.	
"	23.1.17	10 am 12 noon	BOESINGHE VILLAGE & CHATEAU, H.E. & H.V. shells, and our front transport lines bombarded with Reg MINENWERFER, H.E. & H.V. shells. Section Hqr. hut also no damage	

2353 Wt. W2544/1454 700,000 5/15 D. D. & L. A.D.S.S./Forms/C. 2118.

Army Form C. 2118.

WAR DIARY
or
INTELLIGENCE SUMMARY.
(Erase heading not required.)

Instructions regarding War Diaries and Intelligence Summaries are contained in F.S. Regs. Part II. and the Staff Manual respectively. Title pages will be prepared in manuscript.

F-89

Place	Date	Hour	Summary of Events and Information	Remarks and references to Appendices
Lenden.	23.1.17		protested a few Rapidfiring Gun Shells also fell in BOESINGHE. No damage to gun position & no casualties.	
	24.1.17	11 am	3. O.R. proceeded on leave to U.K.	
		11.30 pm	10 L.H.V. Shells fell around 2.1 V.T.M. 10 damage to emplacements but target blocked near 2.1. No casualties.	
	25.1.17	6 am	3 re-enforcements for Base Depot arrived.	
		9.30 am	10 L.H.V. Shell fell around S.'s gun position	
		12 noon	Enemy artillery active against our support line at BOESINGHE VILLAGE.	
	26.1.17	2.30 pm	Lt. Bourton attended conference at Regimental Station	
		5 pm	Advanced position attacked for all guns in the "S" line	
		4.45 pm	Inter-locked volley conducted, further orders to recognise position to be kept in to gun teams month 3/21 ditto sent	
		9 pm	the earlier Defence Scheme – now being issued	
		11.45 pm	2 guns & teams under Lt. Yardley sent to take up emergency position - 1 in BOESINGHE CHURCH + 1 in a house in the MAIN ST. BOESINGHE	
	27.1.17		3 position for protecting our left flank settled – also forward position for guns in Cn.X. line. Work commenced on new position in L7B	

RAILWAY TRENCH

2353 Wt. W2544/1454 700,000 5/15 D.D.&L. A.D.S.S./Forms/C. 2118.

Army Form C. 2118.

WAR DIARY
or
INTELLIGENCE SUMMARY.
(Erase heading not required.)

F. 90

Instructions regarding War Diaries and Intelligence Summaries are contained in F.S. Regs., Part II. and the Staff Manual respectively. Title pages will be prepared in manuscript.

Place	Date	Hour	Summary of Events and Information	Remarks and references to Appendices
London	28.1.17		No special activity.	
	29.1.17	10 am	Working party of 1 N.C.O. & 6 men started work on new position in BRIDGE ST.	
		10 pm	2.O.R.s returned from leave to U.K.	
		11.30 pm	10 L.H.V. Shells fell around the Church – two almost hits being obtained on the mount. Gun position undamaged.	
	30.1.17	1.15 am	The enemy intensely bombarded our immediate left with light howitzers & heavy trench mortars to which our artillery replied vigorously.	
		2.30 am	Work continued on new position for the defence of the X roads and	
		10 pm	our left flank.	
		3 pm	During the bombardment at 1.30 am an S.O.S. signal was observed and our guns at X.1 & X.3 opened fire from _____ on the S.O.S. target, rounds expended 300.	
	31.1.17	3 pm	Inter-section relief. Completed at 6.30 pm. Officers in the line – Lt. Loudon, 2/Lt; Goldberg, 2/Lt; Butler.	
			B.C. in the line – 74.	

W.J. Boughey Lt.
Comdy 115 M.G. Coy

Army Form C. 2118.

WAR DIARY
or
INTELLIGENCE SUMMARY.
(Erase heading not required.)

115 Machine Gun Coy.

Vol 10

FROM
1st FEBRUARY 1917
TO
28th FEBRUARY 1917.

Army Form C. 2118.

E 91.

WAR DIARY
or
INTELLIGENCE SUMMARY.

(Erase heading not required.)

Instructions regarding War Diaries and Intelligence Summaries are contained in F. S. Regs. Part II. and the Staff Manual respectively. Title pages will be prepared in manuscript.

Place	Date	Hour	Summary of Events and Information	Remarks and references to Appendices
Ploegsteert Pecoride Farm	Feb 1st	9am to 2pm	Working party of 1 N.C.O & 6 men on new position on X line	
		9am to	Bombardment of our lines with 18 pdr, 4.2 & 1, 5.9's and French Mortars. No casualties	
		5pm		
	2nd	12.10 pm	1 O.R. killed by sniper at P.4.	
			In retaliation for enemy shelling the enemy bombarded our "S" & "X" lines with 18 pdr, 4.2 & 1, 5.9's. Sniper's and French Mortar. Seven H.E. at Bocangle hit but no damage to Gun positions. Dugouts at S.S. partially destroyed. 3 O.R. wounded.	
	3rd	9am-2pm	Working party on X line positions	
			Our "S" "X" lines & Railway Track bombarded with 4 H.V., 4.2, 26, & Shrapnel. Two direct hits were obtained on our dugout at Z.1. but no damage done. No casualties.	
		6pm to 9pm	Working party on 3/4 & our first line positions	
			During the night 3/4 & we fired 1,000 rounds on	

Army Form C. 2118.

WAR DIARY
or
INTELLIGENCE SUMMARY.
(Erase heading not required.)

Instructions regarding War Diaries and Intelligence Summaries are contained in F.S. Regs., Part II. and the Staff Manual respectively. Title pages will be prepared in manuscript.

F 92

Place	Date	Hour	Summary of Events and Information	Remarks and references to Appendices
Decauville Farm	4/3/16	12 noon to 4 p.m.	CANAL DRIVE, CARIBOO TR. & PALISADE FARM. Working Party with R.E.'s at Pte. St Denis & 3 O.R. returned from H.Q. School, Camiers.	
		11 p.m.	During the night 4/5th we fired 2000 rounds on CANAL DRIVE near CARIBOO TRENCH.	
	5/3/16	8 a.m. to 4 p.m. 9 a.m. to 2 p.m.	Working parties with R.E.'s at P.u & S 3 on "X" line positions.	
	6/3/16		Very quiet day. Working parties as yesterday at P.u, S.Ime, & X line. Enemy batteries engaged in counter battery work in the neighbourhood of ELVERDINGHE.	
	7/3/16		Working parties as yesterday.	
		10 a.m. 6.15 p.m.	10 S.9 shells fell in the area of our camp but no damage done to huts of this unit.	
		7 p.m.	Orders received as to special precaution to be taken in the event of hostile bombardment of camp.	

Army Form C. 2118.

WAR DIARY
or
INTELLIGENCE SUMMARY.
(Erase heading not required.)

F. 9 3

Instructions regarding War Diaries and Intelligence
Summaries are contained in F. S. Regs., Part II.
and the Staff Manual respectively. Title pages
will be prepared in manuscript.

Place	Date	Hour	Summary of Events and Information	Remarks and references to Appendices
~~Poso~~ ~~Estaires~~ ~~Farm~~	4.8.16		Enemy's Artillery very active all day.	
		8 am to 4 pm	Working parties with R.E's at P.4, S.3 mn	
		9.30 pm to 12 mn	Area of Camp bombarded with 5.9's — 15.8	
Decorde Farm			shells being counted. One hut, + Q.m. stores partly destroyed. One mule killed. One Ford ~~car~~ Lorry, portion of limber totally destroyed. Four guns + one hut portion limber + wheels carts badly damaged.	
		2.35 pm to 3 pm	12 5.9's fell in camp. Cook house totally destroyed	
		4.20 pm	2 O.R's killed & 2 wounded. Sapt & P. Nicholson gun shot	
		5 pm	6. 5.9's fell in Camp.	
EMILE FARM.	7.30 pm		Company moved to B.M. 16.1/2 FARM. — B.9. c 70 4.5.	
		9.20 pm	Move completed.	
		7 pm	3 O.R's returned from leave to U.K.	
	9.4.	9 am to 4 pm	18 O.R's working with R.E's at P.4, S.3 mn	
		9 pm — 2 pm	Work continued on "X" line positions.	
			Artillery of both sides active all day	

2353 Wt. W2544/1454 700,000 5/15 D., D. & L. A.D.S.S./Forms/C. 2118.

Army Form C. 2118.

WAR DIARY
or
INTELLIGENCE SUMMARY.
(Erase heading not required.)

F.94.

Instructions regarding War Diaries and Intelligence Summaries are contained in F. S. Regs., Part II. and the Staff Manual respectively. Title pages will be prepared in manuscript.

Place	Date	Hour	Summary of Events and Information	Remarks and references to Appendices
ENIKE FARM	9th Feb		We fired 500 rounds at enemy aeroplane from [post].	
	10.2.16		In BOESINGHE VILLAGE. Working parties as yesterday.	
		9 am	1 O.R. proceeded to England to join an Officer Cadet Unit.	
		9 pm	1 O.R. wounded by M.G. fire at P.4.	
			2/Lt Hales returned from leave (extended) to England	
			2/Lt V. Dunning & 1 O.R. reinforcements	
11.2.16	8 am to 4 pm		Working parties out P.6 & D Lane.	
	9 am – 2 pm		— in respective in X lane	
	12.30 pm		Major Bon returned from leave and resumed command.	
12.7.16			Working parties as yesterday.	
	1 pm		2/Lt Difford returned from Hospital.	
	9.30 am		Some from Gun position shelled but no damage sustained.	
	3.30 pm		Two casualties.	
13.2.16			Working parties as yesterday.	
			Enemy artillery active against our lines with 18pdr, 4.2s, 5.9s.	

Army Form C. 2118.

WAR DIARY
or
INTELLIGENCE SUMMARY.
(Erase heading not required.)

F.95

Instructions regarding War Diaries and Intelligence Summaries are contained in F.S. Regs., Part II. and the Staff Manual respectively. Title pages will be prepared in manuscript.

Place	Date	Hour	Summary of Events and Information	Remarks and references to Appendices
EMILE FARM	July 13		& M.T.M's. About 150 L.H.Y & 4 x5 fell along RAILWAY TRENCH and not beyond at 2.1 was hit twice but not seriously damaged. No casualties.	
	-14		Working parties as yesterday.	
			1.O.R. proceeded to England to join an Officer Cadet Unit	
	-15		Artillery very active throughout night of 14/15th	
			Working parties on new position	
		4 pm	German aeroplane brought down in flames near Coy. H.Q.	
			Inter section relief	
	-16		Working parties as usual.	
	17	9-10 P.M.	30 L.H.Y shells fell around our position at BOESINGHE CH,	
			Artillery activity on both sides.	
		12.30 pm	3 O.R's reinforcements from Base Depôt reported	
	18	7.30 pm	2/Lt Brown to 1.O.R. returned from Divisional School	
			1.O.R. to Corps School	
		10-9 pm	BOESINGHE CH. position shelled with L.H.Y. No damage or casualties sustained.	

Army Form C. 2118.

WAR DIARY
or
INTELLIGENCE SUMMARY.
(Erase heading not required.)

Place	Date	Hour	Summary of Events and Information	Remarks and references to Appendices
EMILE FARM	19.9.16		Enemy unusually quiet all day.	
		9.30pm	Officers reconnoitred "L" line preparing to taking over.	
		6.10pm	He fired 5,000 rounds on RAILWAY CUTTING & trench railway.	
			Enemy searched for our guns with 4.2s	
	20.	9.-10.30am	"S" line position + Church shelled with H.V. Shrapnel - no damage.	
		9am-4pm	Temporary position for P.H. completed.	
			Working parties under R.E. Supervision.	
		6.pm	Company Relieved in BOESINGHE Sector by 196th M.G. Coy	
		11.20pm.	Relief Complete.	
	21st		Occupied "L" line vacated by 196th Coy	
		1.45am.	Relief Complete.	
	22nd	1pm	2/Lt Hillier RFR to 38th Divisional School	
	23rd		Lt. A.M. Smithor appointed at Adjutant.	
			Lt. A. Dunn appointed to Command Gun No. 2. Section.	
	24th		No 11904 Sgt W Ward awarded MILITARY MEDAL by Corps Commander for gallantry at DECOUTE FARM on Feb. 8/17.	

Army Form C. 2118.

WAR DIARY
or
INTELLIGENCE SUMMARY.
(Erase heading not required.)

F. 97

Instructions regarding War Diaries and Intelligence Summaries are contained in F. S. Regs., Part II. and the Staff Manual respectively. Title pages will be prepared in manuscript.

Place	Date	Hour	Summary of Events and Information	Remarks and references to Appendices
~~Hop~~ EMILE	24th	6 pm	Block House positions occupied in accordance with "Defence Scheme - move.	
FARM.		7 pm	Position vacated.	
	25 d			
	26 d			
	27 d		Lt. G. T. Nash returned to duty from sick leave.	
	28 "		Company relieved the 196 d. Coy in the B of S in G H Q Sector	
		8.15 pm	Relief Complete	

J R Bonn Major
Comdg 2/115th M.G. Co

Army Form C. 2118.

WAR DIARY
or
INTELLIGENCE SUMMARY.

(Erase heading not required.)

Vol XI

115th Machine Gun Company.

March 1st to March 31st 1917

Army Form C. 2118.

WAR DIARY
or
INTELLIGENCE SUMMARY.
(Erase heading not required.)

Instructions regarding War Diaries and Intelligence Summaries are contained in F. S. Regs., Part II. and the Staff Manual respectively. Title pages will be prepared in manuscript.

498

Place	Date	Hour	Summary of Events and Information	Remarks and references to Appendices
EMILE FARM	March 3rd		Considerable artillery activity on both sides. Men in reserve camped and revolver practice at ELVERDINGHE. Working parties on new positions.	
			Lt. Yardley attached 1/5 D.R.	
	5th	8 pm	All ranks put through gas chamber with lower box Respirators	
			Intercom relief completed	
	6th		1st Yardley attended VIII Corps School	
	8th		Revolver Practice at ELVERDINGHE	
			2nd D.R. reinforcements arrived	
	10		Company orders stated and the object of counting new Contact Guard	
		7.30pm	Intercommunication relief complete	
		8 pm	Company R.Qm moved to MOUTON FARM B.14.a.2.6	
MOUTON FARM	March 11th	11 am	Working parties — total 21 O.R. on new positions. 2 O.R.s forwarded to VIII Corps Schools.	
		9 pm	Shell hole near B.12.6 prepared as emergency position.	

Army Form C. 2118.

WAR DIARY
or
INTELLIGENCE SUMMARY.
(Erase heading not required.)

F. 99

Instructions regarding War Diaries and Intelligence Summaries are contained in F. S. Regs., Part II. and the Staff Manual respectively. Title pages will be prepared in manuscript.

Place	Date	Hour	Summary of Events and Information	Remarks and references to Appendices
MUTTON FARM.	12 Mar		During night of 11/12th. 2 guns fired on special targets — RAILWAY CUTTING, TELEGRAPH HOUSE & suspected M.Gun. Rounds fired — 6000	
	13 Mar	1.15pm	Enemy artillery active. Observed a very quiet day. At Yeadley attended VIII Corps school for tactical exercise.	
		8.30pm	Working parties on new positions. Enemy artillery again shewed considerable activity.	
	14 Mar		Jimmy and Box Repeaters on practised by all teams in X lines. Working parties on new positions.	
		2pm	Officers Relief carried out.	
			Considerable artillery activity on both sides.	
	15 Mar	1.15pm	Lt Yeadley attended VIII Corps school.	
		3.30pm	Interior Relief carried out.	
	16"		Much artillery & aircraft activity by both sides.	
			Night 15/16th. 2 guns fired on special targets — rounds fired — 3000.	
		2pm	1 O.R. to Divisional Gas School.	
			Working parties on new positions.	

2353   Wt. W2544/1454   700,000   5/15   D. D. & L.   A.D.S.S./Forms/C. 2118.

Army Form C. 2118.

WAR DIARY
or
INTELLIGENCE SUMMARY.
(Erase heading not required.)

Instructions regarding War Diaries and Intelligence Summaries are contained in F. S. Regs., Part II. and the Staff Manual respectively. Title pages will be prepared in manuscript.

F. 1.00

Place	Date	Hour	Summary of Events and Information	Remarks and references to Appendices
MOUTON FARM	16 Mar		Artillery of both sides open active all day	
	17 Mar	1.0pm	An enemy aeroplane over our lines.	
		8.30pm	Band Parade for personnel at M.O. Artillery & trench-mortars open very actively all day	
	18 Mar		Working parties on new positions. Artillery very active all day. Working parties on new positions. One of our guns fired from B.18.a.3.9 in connection with some cutting experiments. 4pm at B.18.a.3.9 ordered to fire day snipers rounds fired — 11.500.	
	19		during return as usual	
		2pm	Officer Relief carried out 4pm at B.18.a.3.9 fired 12,000 during return	
	20	3.30pm	Working parties as usual, between relay carried out.	

2353 Wt. W2544/1454 700,000 5/15 D. D. & L. A.D.S.S.JForms/C. 2118.

Army Form C. 2118.

WAR DIARY or INTELLIGENCE SUMMARY.

(Erase heading not required.)

Instructions regarding War Diaries and Intelligence Summaries are contained in F. S. Regs., Part II. and the Staff Manual respectively. Title pages will be prepared in manuscript.

F.107

Place	Date	Hour	Summary of Events and Information	Remarks and references to Appendices
MOUTON FARM	21st		Artillery fairly active all day. Working parties as usual.	
	22nd	6.15 p.m.	Heavy artillery bombardment on our right lasting until 6.30 am. S.O.S. signal given. Working parties as usual. Gun at B.12 a 3.9 Fired 7,000 rounds. Order to leave for received at 9.30 pm. Extract from Corps Order dated 21.3.17 "Temp 2/Lt R.C Golding to be temp Lieut 1.1.17"	
	23rd		Generally quiet. Sniper artillery activity by both sides. 2/Lt Miller + 2 O.R. from 38th Div School	
	24th	3 pm	Officers Relief Carried out. Artillery + Trench Mortar fairly active all day. We fired "Gun from B.11.4.9.7 at hostile aeroplane – 320 rds	
	25th	2 pm	2/Lt Davies to 38th Div Lys School	

Army Form C. 2118.

F. 102

WAR DIARY
or
INTELLIGENCE SUMMARY.
(Erase heading not required.)

Instructions regarding War Diaries and Intelligence Summaries are contained in F. S. Regs., Part II. and the Staff Manual respectively. Title pages will be prepared in manuscript.

Place	Date	Hour	Summary of Events and Information	Remarks and references to Appendices
MOUTON FARM.	25.	3.30pm.	Inspection Relief carried out. Programme of work under R.E. Supervision continued. Enemy's aircraft active. Also many Traction Engines up. Artillery less active.	
	26.	3pm	Heavy bombardment by Belgians on our left. Lasting until 4pm.	
		6am	15th H.W. Welsh & Grantham ???. Base Depot. Very little activity all day. Working parties as usual.	
	27.		Artillery more active today mainly H.M.V. Shrapnel.	
		6.15pm	Two of our planes flying very high over enemys lines. Heavy shelled by A.A. Guns but all returned.	
	28.		1 O.R. returned from leave G.H.K. Working parties on new position from 7.30am-12.30 & 11.30pm-6.30pm in front of battle portion R.12.6.	
	29.	8pm	Partly of 1 O.R. commenced work. Officers Relief carried out.	
		3pm	2 O.R's to Divl & Army Schools of Instruction.	

2353 Wt. W3541/1454 700,000 5/15 D. D. & L. A.D.S.S./Forms/C. 2118.

WAR DIARY
or
INTELLIGENCE SUMMARY

Army Form C. 2118.

Place	Date	Hour	Summary of Events and Information	Remarks and references to Appendices
MOUTON FARM	29th Apr.	3 pm	4 Para 4 OR. from Point Ypr Cebal. Working Parties on new position	
	30.4.	3.30 pm	Later section relief carried out at 2/2. D.G. Dyfleck struck strength (less to England). Working parties on new position. New Dugout operation for B.12.2 & B.12.3 occupied	
	31.4	10 am	Billets inspected by G.O.C. 38th Division. 2/2. drillers passed by No. 1 Section rue 2/2. Dyfleck. J.M. activity during the morning. Neighbourhood of M.G. B.12.1 bombarded. Quantity of dugouts destroyed. Duckwalks	

W. Bonfrey Lt
OC No 2 Coy
115

Army Form C. 2118.

WAR DIARY
INTELLIGENCE SUMMARY

(Erase heading not required.)

Place	Date	Hour	Summary of Events and Information	Remarks and references to Appendices
MOUTON FARM	1 April 17	11 AM	C of E Service held in camp.	
			Smoking Parties on manufacture - 20 O.R.	
			No special activity on our front.	
	2 April	10 am	Kit Inspection Parade	
		12 noon	Working Parties - as before	
			Slight Artillery activity all day. Trench activity on L.C. an	
	3 April	12 noon	Working Parties continued	
		3 pm	Officers Relief Carried out	
		4 pm	Usual hostile bombardment of Telm & neighbourhood of M.G.B 15.1.	
		4.30 pm	No. 2 Bowling Post destroyed. 2 O.R. wounded by shrapnel near ELVERDINGHE (one remained at duty.)	
			N.C.O. i/c B.12.1. placed under arrest (report of Bng. General)	
	4 April	noon	Working Parties continued	
			Interstocks Relief carried out.	
		3 pm	L. Cumberit. Shelling all day.	
	5 April	11 pm	3 O.R. Reinforcements from Base Depot arrived	

Army Form C. 2118.

WAR DIARY
or
INTELLIGENCE SUMMARY.
(Erase heading not required.)

F. 18.5

Instructions regarding War Diaries and Intelligence Summaries are contained in F. S. Regs., Part II. and the Staff Manual respectively. Title pages will be prepared in manuscript.

Place	Date	Hour	Summary of Events and Information	Remarks and references to Appendices
MOUTON FARM	4/15	noon	Working parties continued	
		3 pm	Sgt Bryce proceeded to England to join Officer Cadet School	
	5/15	—	1 OR to the army School of Cookery	
		10 pm	2 Officers returned to "Y" A.A. Battery for instruction in shooting aeroplanes	
		noon	Working parties continued	
	6/15	—	—	
		—	Slight artillery activity all day	
	7/15	noon	Working parties continued	
	8		EASTER SUNDAY	
		3 pm	Officers Relief arrived at	
	9	noon	Working parties continued	
		3.30 pm	Subalterns relief carried out	
			Slight artillery activity	
	10	noon	Working parties continued	
		3 pm	2 OR working at M.G. B.17.1 wounded with Rifle grenade	

Army Form C. 2118.

WAR DIARY
or
INTELLIGENCE SUMMARY.
(Erase heading not required.)

F.106.

Place	Date	Hour	Summary of Events and Information	Remarks and references to Appendices
MOUTON FARM	Apl 10	6.30pm	2/Lt. Bean reinforcement from Base Depot arrived. 1.O.R.	
	Apl 11		2/Lt D.Sevier reinforcement from A.H.T.D. arrived. 1 O.R. reinforcement from F.G.C.M. assembled at Comn H.Q. MOUTON FARM	
	" 12	11 am		
	" 13	3 pm	Officers Relief carried out. 2/Lt Geo London to Dental Hospital Boulogne. 1.O.R. to VIII Corps School.	
		4 pm	Commanding Officer made a reconnaissance of front line & select 6 gun positions	
	" 14	3.30 pm	Intervalin relief carried out	
	" 15		New emplacement at M.G. B 12.1 Completed & occupied. Considerable enemy T.M. activity on both sides.	
	" 16		Work on emplacements on new positions	
	" 17		Officers Relief carried out	

Army Form C. 2118.

WAR DIARY
or
INTELLIGENCE SUMMARY
(Erase heading not required.)

F/107

Place	Date	Hour	Summary of Events and Information	Remarks and references to Appendices
MOUTON FARM	Apl 19		Inspection. Relief carried out.	
	20		Work in new position continued.	
			Test of new muzzle cups carried out. 3 new rounds fired. Cups found to be quite satisfactory, no stoppages or breakages being experienced.	
	21		2/Lt London proceeded to Chinese Labour Corps Y. Struck off strength of company.	
			Sgt Lewis (gun no 1) E.S.R. during the storm.	
	21		C.S.M. Healy.	
			Neighbourhood of Z.2.1. Enemy patrols shelled with L.H.V.	
	22		V.H.E. 2 rounds no casualties sustained.	
	2-3		1 O.R. to VIII Corps Rest of Battalion.	
	24		Officers Relief carried out. Our Artillery active in enemy's support all day. Intensive Relief carried out. Enemy bombarded 10 pm to 10.30 pm intermittently S.O.S. signal	
	25		Set up in night Divisional Sector. Two reinforcements arrive at Reinforcement Camp	
			C.S.M. Healy evacuated.	

WAR DIARY
INTELLIGENCE SUMMARY
(Erase heading not required.)

Army Form C. 2118.

F.108.

Place	Date	Hour	Summary of Events and Information	Remarks and references to Appendices
MOUTON FM.	April 1917 25.		Sjt. Neville M. appointed acting Company Serjeant Major vice C.S.M. Healey evacuated	
	26	6 p.m.	Gun teams reinforced to 1 N.C.O. and 6 men per team.	
			Lieut. W. T. Boughey proceeds to U.K. under authority A.G.'s letter A/2322 of 23.4.17.	
			2nd Lieut. R. THOMPSON arrives to replace Lieut. Boughey.	
	27		Drill and exceptionally quiet day in the line	
	28		2nd Lieut. N.A.B. Miller to Hospital. Our heavy artillery active on enemy supports all day.	
	29		C.O. and O.C. of 176 M.G.Coy makes a reconnaissance of route prior to relief.	
			2nd Lieut Miller and 5 men proceed to CASSIERS en route for instruction.	
		9.30 p.m.	Bombardment of "CAESAR'S NOSE" (enemy machine) carried out	
	30	12.30 a.m.	Both sides active with artillery.	
		K1.30 a.m.		
			Lieut. Davis and men on proceed to MILLAIN Killed for Company.	
		1.30 p.m.	2nd Lieut Thompson and 2 men proceed to 3rd M. Aerial School en route for instruction.	

[signature]

Army Form C. 2118.

WAR DIARY

~~INTELLIGENCE~~ SUMMARY.

(Erase heading not required.)

Vol 13

115 Machine Gun Company.

May 1st to May 31st 1917.

Army Form C. 2118.

Instructions regarding War Diaries and Intelligence
Summaries are contained in F. S. Regs., Part II.
and the Staff Manual respectively. Title pages
will be prepared in manuscript.

WAR DIARY
INTELLIGENCE SUMMARY

(Erase heading not required.)

7109.

Place	Date	Hour	Summary of Events and Information	Remarks and references to Appendices
MOUTON FM.	1917 May. 1	2 p.m.	Company Relief begun.	
		8.30 p.m.	Company relieved in the line by No. 176 Machine Gun Company. Heavy counter battery artillery work by enemy during the day. Aircraft very active.	
	2	5 a.m.	Company moved from MOUTON FM. to POPERINGHE and entrained there at 7 a.m. for ESQUELBEC. Arrived there 11 a.m. and marched to MILLAIN. Transport trouble by road leaving at 4 a.m. and arriving MILLAIN at 4 p.m. 1 Officer and 7 O.R.s with kit proceeded by Motor Lorries leaving MOUTON FM. at 7.15 a.m. and arriving MILLAIN at 11.30 a.m.	
MILLAIN	3	7 a.m.	Training begun. All Lewis Gun stores checked and distributed and cleaned. Two reinforcements reported.	
"	4	9 a.m. to 1 p.m.	Tactical training carried out on Brigade Training Ground. Advancing to contact, and to action from Lewis practised.	
"	5	9.45 a.m.	Inspection of Company's Billets by O.C. 115th Bde.	
		11 a.m.	No. 48846 Pte. Pound R.O. RAM.C. tried by F.G.C.M. Charge "Neglect to the prejudice of good order and military discipline." Finding "Guilty". Sentence 'To undergo 90 days F.P. Ns. I.' Confirmed by G.O.C. 115th Bde. 6.5.1917.	
		4.30 p.m.	Company Drill and Run Drill practised in parade ground. Company Association Football Team beat Bde. H.Q. and TMB. Team in Recreational Training Cup. Ground.	CTM

2353 Wt W:354/1454 700,000 5/15 D. D. & L.   A.D.S.S./Forms/C. 2118.

Army Form C. 2118.

WAR DIARY or INTELLIGENCE SUMMARY.

(Erase heading not required.)

Instructions regarding War Diaries and Intelligence Summaries are contained in F. S. Regs., Part II. and the Staff Manual respectively. Title pages will be prepared in manuscript.

7/10

Place	Date	Hour	Summary of Events and Information	Remarks and references to Appendices
MILLAIN	1917 May 6	11.0 a.m.	Church of England Service for whole Brigade held on the Training Ground.	
			R.C. Service in MILLAIN Church at 11 am and Nonconformist Service at 9 am.	
	7	12 mid day	Church post G.O.C. Bde after Service at 12 midday.	
		9 am	Route march.	
			Probable taking up position on the way. Returned 1.30 pm	
		2.30	Cleaned & reluricated arms & prepared Equipment Return	
	8	8.45 a	Company proceeded to Range, fires Pos'l Lelle C.	
		2.0 pm	Divisional Lectures Officers on Anti-Aircraft M.G. work.	
		3.0pm	Company Drill	
	9	9.0	Company parade in full fighting kit with limbers & proceed to the Training Area & practice Wood fighting.	
		2-3 pm	Midinners & Clinary	
		3.40	Lecture by Colonel Officers on the Learning Rifle - Thursday Drill.	
	10	9.12 am	Section proceeded to Pritshem for practising attack No 2 & 4 th 11.7 to B. No 4 & 17 th Bn.	
		12.30 pm	No 1 section now attached to 16th Welch No 3 to 10 at Gas On	
			Company parade out with 1st Royal Fus Externan	
		3.30	Service for R.C. soldiers in MILLAIN Church	A.K.S.

T.134. Wt. W708—776. 500000. 4/15. Sir J. C. & S.

WAR DIARY
or
INTELLIGENCE SUMMARY.
(Erase heading not required.)

Army Form C. 2118.

F.111

Instructions regarding War Diaries and Intelligence Summaries are contained in F.S. Regs., Part II. and the Staff Manual respectively. Title pages will be prepared in manuscript.

Place	Date	Hour	Summary of Events and Information	Remarks and references to Appendices
MILLAIN	1917 May 11	7-11am	Nos 1&2 Section attended the Range for Revolver practice	
		9pm	No 3 Section no returned to 10 S.W.B. to practice in which G.O.C. 38th Division present	
		9-230	1&4 Section now attached to 17th R.W.F. Company Sports Meeting held. Brass Depot	
			Three reinforcements arrived as Reinforcement Coys from Base Depot	
	12	5.30-7.30	Nos 1 & 2 Section were attached to the 16th Welsh. G.O.C. 2nd Army present	
		2pm-4.30	Nos 3&4 Section were attached to 10 S.W.B. to practice in which Revolver on stage	
			G.O.C. 2nd Army present	
	13th	10.30	Church Parade for C.E. at MILLAIN at 11.0. R.C. MILLAIN CH at 11.0am	
		9.0	Noncoformists at 11/ 10th R.W.F. Transport held a gymkhana	
		1.00	Brigade Sports held at Training Area. M.G. limber arrived Special Base	
			Company's Rations distributed. Field suspension belt	
			2nd Lieut. H.A.B. Miller evacuated to 15th C.C.S.	
	14th	9.0	No 3&4 Sectn attached to 11th S.W.B. for practising the attack	
		12.30	No 1&2 " " " 17th R.W.F " " "	
			Wind helmets issued & masks	
	15th	9.am	Company participated in Brigade attack 12 gas going through five types from	ac/g

T134. Wt. W708—776. 500000. 4/15. Sir J. C. & S.

Army Form C. 2118.

F112

WAR DIARY
or
INTELLIGENCE SUMMARY.
(Erase heading not required.)

Instructions regarding War Diaries and Intelligence Summaries are contained in F. S. Regs., Part II. and the Staff Manual respectively. Title pages will be prepared in manuscript.

Place	Date	Hour	Summary of Events and Information	Remarks and references to Appendices
MILLAIN	1917 May 15	8.30am	Enemy shwick firm & subsequently going forward & consolidating positions gained	
	16	7.15	Company moved back to the Herzeele line, arrived there at 12.30	
			Men left behind to try to recover stores in Millain camp on the 15th	
			Tent inspection held	
HERZEELE	17th	4pm	Company moved to Y Camp Poperinghe arrived there at 6.30pm G.O.C. 32nd Div	
			was on the line of route & inspected the Column.	
	18th	9.0am	Company moved to MORTON FARM, ELVERDINGHE	
		3.30pm	Relieved 176 Company on the BOESINGHE sector. Relief completed by 10.30pm	
			Enemy shelled battery positions in ELVERDINGHE	
			Major Bone attached to Hospital	
	19th		Enemy shelled batteries in BRIELEN and ELVERDINGHE. Our artillery active all day	
			in Counter Battery work. Aircraft active. Major Bone from Hospital	
	20th	11am	Church Parade. Service at ELVERDINGHE	
			ELVERDINGHE battery heavily shelled. Enemy shelling nothing all day by both sides	
			Major Bone to M.G. School Camiers. 2 O. Ranks returned from M.G. School Camiers	
	21st		Work commenced on new Company H.Q. for men at (Gobtein B.14.a.4.0.1.5)	a.c.f.

T2134. Wt. W708—776. 500000. 4/15. Sir J. C. & S.

Army Form C. 2118.

F 113

WAR DIARY
or
INTELLIGENCE SUMMARY.
(Erase heading not required.)

Place	Date	Hour	Summary of Events and Information	Remarks and references to Appendices
MOULTON FARM	21/5/17		Heavy casualties to working party. Casualties shelled until 10.30 am among F.W. in trenches.	
	22/5/17	9.0 am	Working Party at Steenwerch. 2nd Lt. Watts shells returned from R.E. C.O.	
		10.0	Tackled heavy farm as by P.R. Two reinforcements arrived	
			Enemy shelled back area of BRIELEN & ELVERDINGHE. Our light shelled the forward area.	
	23/5/17	8.0 am	Working Party at Ferme Cot.	
		9 am	March Coy 14 F... to be billets ELVERDINGHE CHATEAU. Enemy shells BOESINGHE	
			Intr. to 2nd Relief duty carried out.	
		10.5 am during considerable change.	
	24/5/17	6.0 am	Working Party at Ferme Cot.	
		10.45	Enemy shelled battery in rear of Coy H.Q. several shells falling on 6 in. H.E.'s battery.	
			Officer Pattern also changed by our men & Lt. Major sen. Officers to change	
			Two men killed whilst going off the line with rations. This morning wounded.	
	25/5/17	8.0 am	Working Party at Ferme Cot.	
		10.30	The funeral of the two men killed this morning was little the H.E. Gravekerk offered.	
			Enemy artillery very active and shelling trenches.	

Army Form C. 2118.

WAR DIARY
or
INTELLIGENCE SUMMARY.
(Erase heading not required.)

Instructions regarding War Diaries and Intelligence Summaries are contained in F. S. Regs., Part II. and the Staff Manual respectively. Title pages will be prepared in manuscript.

F 114

Place	Date	Hour	Summary of Events and Information	Remarks and references to Appendices
NORTH FARM	26.5.17	8am	Working Party at Trenches OK	
		7.45am	Enemy aeroplane sighted by H.Q. and fired at ELVERDINGHE.	
			Enemy again shelled BOESINGHE with 15cm & 10cm heavy howitzer batteries	
	27.5.17	2am	Working Party as usual at Trenches OK	
		10am	Church of England service at NORTH FARM. Holy Communion afterwards	
			Enemy shelled back areas	
	28.5.17	8am	Working Party in Trenches OK as usual. Light hostile artillery activity	
			Inter Section Relief carried out	
	29.5.17		Most successful raid by proposed CO's C.S.M. party accompanied by Engineers C.S.M. Heavy hostile Counter Battery work. Aerial activity	
	30.5.17		Working Party at Trenches as usual. Lieut. Muir attended a demonstration of	
			Mills, L.M. & Stokes. One reinforcement arrived from 115 Sy. Battalion	
	31.5.17		Work still proceeding at Trenches OK. T.M. Bombardment carried out on OXU	
			DRIVE. Protective barrage carried out by Divisional Artillery on Outpost Coln.	
			Trenches.	
			Night firing. Spurs going heavy fire or enemy communication.	
			25 OTT Lewis fired. One casualty (wounded)	

C.M.Hale. Lieut. Comdg 20.g
O.C. 115 Machine Gun Co

T2134. Wt. W708—776. 500000. 4/15. Sir J. C. & S.

Army Form C. 2118.

WAR DIARY
or
INTELLIGENCE SUMMARY.
(*Erase heading not required.*)

Vol 14

115 Machine Gun Company

1st June to 30th June 1917

Army Form C. 2118.

F.115

WAR DIARY
or
INTELLIGENCE SUMMARY.
(Erase heading not required.)

Instructions regarding War Diaries and Intelligence Summaries are contained in F. S. Regs., Part II. and the Staff Manual respectively. Title pages will be prepared in manuscript.

Place	Date	Hour	Summary of Events and Information	Remarks and references to Appendices
MARTINPUICH	1-6-17	8.0 am	NFA moved in at new by HQ at FRENCH CoY. 2nd Lieut. Lakin reported to Enemy shelled forward first area during the day. Enemy's front & strafe area near M.GUN down near WIBITSI Redan	
	2-6-17		Work commenced on 2nd M.G. Emplacement at CANAL BANK North & late 28N u 2 c 33 & Enemy's shelled BECOURT plus being worked at V.RAPPORTE. Our artillery respecter all day.	
	3-6-17		2 Lt Thompson arrived. Listen however relied	
	4-6-17	3.0 pm	Practic barrage carried out. All fields put Every front positions. Enemy retaliated on M.G. site on Tower Hamlets Ridge & Ave Gallant & Lt Ingram with 3 O.R.'s temporarily [...] bullets in 1 hour. Gas Alarm sounded.	
	5-6-17	10 am	Enemy shelled BECOURT & [...] & Lining [...]	
		5.0	Enemy heavy shelled SHEER ELVERDINGE CHATEAU & around. 1 Reinforcement arrived.	
	6-6-17		Forward area quiet. Bad news this morning that Enemy Relay Emplacement	
	6-6-17		Lieut. Davies & Hospital had been destroyed during Tuesday's strafe.	
			Corporal Lidell Ongar reported To enemy Radar of the	
			16th Welch admitted wounded. To severe an enemy trench. On cavalry	
			1 Officer [...] [...] & guidelines positive shot about by our planes [...] [...] [...]	

Army Form C. 2118.

F.116

WAR DIARY
or
INTELLIGENCE SUMMARY.
(Erase heading not required.)

Instructions regarding War Diaries and Intelligence Summaries are contained in F. S. Regs., Part II. and the Staff Manual respectively. Title pages will be prepared in manuscript.

Place	Date	Hour	Summary of Events and Information	Remarks and references to Appendices
No 37 and 9/6/17			Inter-Bation relief carried out. Was reinforcing repulsed	
			Boncourt Ridge. Wire Company at 5/6th Joints. All the were 1000 yards front	
			M.G. fire very heavy continued	
			Lieut D Davis wounded. Now & placed 4th relieved of Company. No Bons 11b	
	8.6.17		Enemy shells forward.	
	9.6.17		Artillery during the day rather stellar, Wire & Gun Cloud to Reinf. Fronz 10 Bombs	
			X Line a line station	
	10.6.17		Forward and between of OH's very strong	
	11.6.17		Artillery & M.G. fire an ex day very heavy. Hand shells in room	
	12.6.17		Lpls. Nelson relief carried out. Gunshot wound in shoulder	
	13.6.17		68634 Pte Brockwood wounded 11/6/17. Slightly of moved that should rifle	
			Enemy shells forward area. Recommended by W. Inspir hill by	
	14.6.17		Pte Elson lt-duty Corporal 11.6.17. Slightly very artily active	
			Enemy artillery very active all day in forward area. Borough Elson & Nelson heavy shell	
			L/C Bryant (Transport) to be acting Corporal (unpaid). Pte Robinson to be Lpl. (unpaid).	
			Pte Reynolds Feutlin wounded on duty Cpl R.A.M.C. aerograph 9 echo	
			admitted from 11th June 1917. Contained W.B.T.O.O.C. 115 Inftry Support attend 14.6.17 L.C. 2020	
	15.6.17			

T2134. Wt. W708—776. 600000. 4/15. Sir J. C. & S.

Army Form C. 2118.

F.117

WAR DIARY
or
INTELLIGENCE SUMMARY.
(Erase heading not required.)

Place	Date	Hour	Summary of Events and Information	Remarks and references to Appendices
MOULTON FARM	15.6.17		Enemy shelled forward & back areas all day. Our artillery fired in reply throughout anon.	
	16.6.17		Pte Walton (No 25127) from M.M. (unconscious) Enemy artillery very active at night with harassing fire shelling route to Bridges & M.G. lines along Elverdinghe Cross Road. 32 men attached to G from Infantry	
	17.6.17		Company relieved on the BOESINGHE SECTOR by the 2nd Canadian Bayais M.G Coy (Capt Wright) Relief successfully carried out. Great deal care of the pa'n harried by shell fire, enemy notice. Fairly quiet day.	
Vof Vaci	18.6.17		Cleaning guns & fire kits. Working Party at night carrying M.G. emplacements. Improvements carried out from Rubbers Camp. 27094 Pte Gripping evacuated.	
	19.6.17	6.30am	Reveille 6.30am. Breakfast 7.0am.	
		9.0.	Checking spare Parts	
		2pm	Inspection Pulls. — Work commenced to 9am & 10-9.1	
	20.6.17		Morning Parades under Section Officers. Afternoon Lecture Demonstration by Section Officers on Lewisian Lights, Beers & No 9.1" Box Carriage emergency equipt.	
	21.6.17	9.0am	Physical training. 9.20am–11.30 Cleaning Kit at 12.0 Inspection of guns & kit by C.O.	
		2pm	Kit inspection. Pte Mayll G. & Pte Bull H. be boys evac L/cpl. On Bouquet exercise L.C.S	

Army Form C. 2118.

F 118

WAR DIARY
or
INTELLIGENCE SUMMARY.
(Erase heading not required.)

Instructions regarding War Diaries and Intelligence Summaries are contained in F. S. Regs., Part II. and the Staff Manual respectively. Title pages will be prepared in manuscript.

Place	Date	Hour	Summary of Events and Information	Remarks and references to Appendices
Vox Vrai A.10.b.2	22/6/17	9 a.m.	Physical Training 20 C.O. inspection 2.15-2.50 Gas Drill 3-4 p.m. Inoculation Below	
	23/6/17	9 a.m.	Company Parade 9.15-10 a.m. Physical Training 10.15-11.15 Gas Drill 11.20-12 Lempohm under 3/Lt P. Barnes. 12-12.45. Instruction in care & cleaning 1-3 pm Mechanism by Gun Team Commanders. 3-4 pm Immediate Reparts also Lt P. for instruction to attached Infantry men. Work completed on M.G. Emplacement Church Parade.	
	24/6/17	9.20	Work finished in construction of dam at A.10.a.91. Enemy aeroplane flew low over camp at 3.30 am. Very heavy fire & reported to have been brought down.	
	25/6/17	9 a.m.	Company Parade 9.15-10.30. Physical Training & Rifle Exercises 10.30-11.15 Semaphores. 11.30-12.30 Gas Drill. 2-4 pm Range (Fonkay) + fist inspection. Instruction of attached men carried out. Enemy plane flying low over camp at 6 pm.	
	26/6/17	9 a.m.	Company Parade 9.15-10.30 am Physical Training & Rifle exercises 10.45-11.15 Semaphore 11.30-12.30 Cleaning Guns. 2.30-4.30 pm Packing Limbers - Camp Fatigues. Two reinforcements arrived on from O.C.S. + one from Reinforcement Camp. 113974 Pte Webb S to acting L/Corporal (Unpaid).	
	27/6/17	7 a.m.	Company Paraded to transport moved to Foster, these continued marched to Couet	

Army Form C. 2118.

WAR DIARY
or
INTELLIGENCE SUMMARY.
(Erase heading not required.)

Instructions regarding War Diaries and Intelligence Summaries are contained in F. S. Regs., Part II. and the Staff Manual respectively. Title pages will be prepared in manuscript.

F.11 9

Place	Date	Hour	Summary of Events and Information	Remarks and references to Appendices
CAESTRE	27.6.17	1.0 am	Arrived at Caestre before the troops following. Very heavy fall of rain during the afternoon & evening.	
			Fine reinforcement arrived today at 38th Div. Reinforcement Camp from Base Depot.	
	28.6.17	7.0	Company paraded & marched off to embussing point	
		8.30	Left Caestre by bus & journeyed to FEBVIN-PALFART via HAZEBROUCK STEENVOORDE AIRE.	
FEBVIN-PALFART		12.30 pm	Arrived at FEBVIN-PALFART and billeted by Billeting Officer & others in anticipated time to their respective billets.	
	29.6.17	6.0 am	Reveille. 7.30 am Breakfast. 9.0 Company Parade. 9.15-10.15 Company Drill. 10-11 Closing Arms Drill. 11.30-12.30 Physical Training - Swedish (half Company). 2 pm to 4 pm Instruction & Demonstration on duties of Section Commander in Open Warfare. Classes to be for Instructional training of N.C.O.s & Men and completion of Registrations.	
			7 O. C. M. Released 2.5 12.11th Welch. N. R. C. Godfrey acted as prisoner. Lt. Simpson as Prisoners Escort. Lt. Hale governed.	
	30.6.17	6.0 am	Reveille. 7-7.45 am Breakfast. 9.15-10.15 Auditory Musketry Drill. 9 am C.O. Inspection 10.15 to 11 Physical Training (Swedish). 11.30-12.30 Smoke Drill. Settled 23.11 12 Welch, 30 days F. P. No. 1 - Refused all performance of Duties.	

A. C. Godfrey Major
a. O. C. 115 Machine Gun Coy
30/6/17

Army Form C. 2118.

Nov 15

WAR DIARY
or
INTELLIGENCE SUMMARY.
(Erase heading not required.)

115th Company.

Machine Gun Corps.

War Diary.

1st to 31st July 1917.

Army Form C. 2118.

WAR DIARY
or
INTELLIGENCE SUMMARY.
(Erase heading not required.)

F. 120

Instructions regarding War Diaries and Intelligence Summaries are contained in F.S. Regs., Part II. and the Staff Manual respectively. Title pages will be prepared in manuscript.

Place	Date	Hour	Summary of Events and Information	Remarks and references to Appendices
FERVIN-PALFART	1914 JULY 1	9 a.m.	Church of England Parade Service on 16th Battn. Welsh Regt. parade ground.	
		9.30 a.	Nonconformist Parade.	
		9.45 a	Roman Catholic Parade: service in FERVIN-PALFART Church	
			Day devoted to cleaning up, settling into billets, and preparing for training.	
"	2	4 a.m.	Training begins. Squad Drill till 4.45 a.m.	
		9 a.m.	C.O.'s Inspection followed by Rough Grazing and Company Drill.	
		2–4 p.m.	Bell-filling competition. Two men per section provided on leave of Stretcher bearing.	
			Company Willetted near some Portuguese Regiments into carried out artillery practice on Wk 12·9	
"	3	6 p.m.	The Commanding Officer Major F.A.F. Bone returned from leave to U.K.	
		4.45	Squad Drill. Nos. 1 & 2 Sections proceeded to range all day and carried out practice	
"		9 a.m. at 200ˣ range. Nos. 3 & 4 Sections carried out Elementary Drill and practice. Immediate			
		4 p.m.	Action and Bell-filling.	
			Extract from 5th A.R.O. of 29.6.1914. "The Army Commander wishes to express his appreciation	
			of the following act of courage on the part of G. No. 25111 Lance Corporal T.H. Taylor, 115th Coy,	
			"Machine Gun Corps. On 16th Nov. June 1917, a pair of horses attached to a limber wagon	
			"bolted along a main thoroughfare. Lance Corporal Taylor, who was mounted, galloped	
			"after them, and when level with them, gathered up the reins, bringing them to a halt within a ⟨GTH⟩	

T2134. Wt. W708—776. 500000. 4/15. Sir J.C. & S.

Army Form C. 2118.

WAR DIARY
or
INTELLIGENCE SUMMARY.
(Erase heading not required.)

F. 121.

Instructions regarding War Diaries and Intelligence Summaries are contained in F. S. Regs., Part II. and the Staff Manual respectively. Title pages will be prepared in manuscript.

Place	Date	Hour	Summary of Events and Information	Remarks and references to Appendices
FEBVIN-PALFART	1919 July 3	(cont.)	"few rounds of a six horsed wagon team. There was considerable traffic at the time, and his action involved a considerable amount of personal risk. Award of Medaille not made in the Regimental Orders." Sheet of Lance Corporal Taylor in accordance with "Para. 1919 (XIV) Kings Regulations."	
	4	9 a.m.	Five Reinforcements arrived from Base Depot. Sgt. Ward & 3 men returned from Army Rest Camp. Brigade Training. Beforenoon Company with Fighting Limbers and Cookers Cart out west carried out detail training Inspection, proceeding, siting of supporting and close	
		5 p.m.	watering line, also concealment in the Grave. Company returned to billets. Dinners 8.30.	
			Two Reinforcements arrived from Base Depot.	
	5	7 a.m.	Squad Drill till 4.5 a.m.	
		9 a.m. to 4 p.m.	Gun Drill, Sight setting and laying, and overhauling of all belts.	
	6	6 a.m. to 4 p.m.	Brigade Training on the Area allotted, and day with specimen trenches. The employment of troops in the forthcoming operations practised. Divisional Commander present.	
	7	7 a.m. to 5 p.m.	Brigade Training day by day, carried out. Operation practising troops in work. One section consolidating, two in Brigade reserve.	(GTH)

T2134. Wt. W708—776. 500000. 4/15. Sir J. C. & S.

Army Form C. 2118.

F. 122

WAR DIARY
or
INTELLIGENCE SUMMARY.
(Erase heading not required.)

Place	Date	Hour	Summary of Events and Information	Remarks and references to Appendices
FEBVIN-PALFART	1914 July 7	(cont)	Sgt. Burford appointed C.Q.M.S. of 149 M.G. Co. Struck off strength accordingly. One other rank granted leave to U.K. 8th to 18th.	
	8	9 a.m.	Church of England Parade service.	
		9.30 a.m.	Roman Catholic Service in FEBVIN-PALFART Church.	
		11 a.m.	Nonconformist service.	
			Rest day, devoted to cleaning up and a rest. One attached man went to Hospital.	
	9	7-7.45 a.m.	Squad Drill.	
		9 a.m. to 12.30 p.m.	Instruction and demonstration in the use of Yukon Packs and Pack Saddlery, and in the writing of messages and reports.	
		3 p.m.	Inspection of the Company by the General Officer Commanding 115th Brigade. The company was drawn up in hicks with full transport, and demonstration in driving, and range finding were given. The limbers and spare parts were also inspected.	
	10	9.30 a.m. to 4.30 p.m.	Brigade Training in special area. Half Brigade practised last stage of withdrawing operations. Coveringparties and rations in contact attack practised. Pack saddlery and Yukon Packs used. One driver and one attached man to Hospital.	

Army Form C. 2118.

F. 123.

WAR DIARY
or
INTELLIGENCE SUMMARY.
(Erase heading not required.)

Place	Date	Hour	Summary of Events and Information	Remarks and references to Appendices
FEBVIN-PALFART	1917 Jan 11	9 am	Inspection of Box Respirators and P.H. Helmets. All steel helmets painted and sprinkled	
		10	with sand for invisibility purposes. Belt filling in the field, and instructors in	
		4 pm	the writing of messages and reports practised.	
	12	6 am	Company moved off to Training Area for Divisional Training.	
		9 am	Zero hour. Practice attack begun. 115th Bde in Reserve. Pick & Shovel Battery exercises	
			under orders of Brigade Transport Officer. Barrage taken practice under	
			orders of Divisional Machine Gun Officer.	
		4 pm	Operations finish. Conference held by G.O.C. 115th Bde. at 6 pm Company bivouacked	
			in Training Area.	
	13	1:30 am	Company moved off to practise the attack at dawn.	
		3:29 am	Zero Hour. Two Battns did barrage work. One section practised consolidation	
			on a area forced flanking oppose for strong points.	
		6 am	Operations cease. Breakfast on Training Area.	
		8 pm	Conference by G.O.C. 115th Bde. after which M. Brigade were formed up in mass,	
			and the B.G.C. reviewed upon the progress made by the Brigade during Training (OTM)	
		1 pm	Company arrived back in billets.	

Army Form C. 2118.

F.124.

WAR DIARY
or
INTELLIGENCE SUMMARY.
(Erase heading not required.)

Instructions regarding War Diaries and Intelligence Summaries are contained in F.S. Regs., Part II. and the Staff Manual respectively. Title pages will be prepared in manuscript.

Place	Date	Hour	Summary of Events and Information	Remarks and references to Appendices
FEBVIN- PALFART	1919 July 14	9 am	Commanding Officers inspection parade.	
		9.15 am	Inspection of all hands held by C.O. After this kind, yesterday in charge of party practising smoke starting antwerpe. Immediate action, and practice impromptu exercises; also issue of pinafores. Two reinforcements arrived from Base Depôt. One man from Hospital. Two men evacuated. One N.C.O forward to Cadet School, England. Two men to Hospital.	
	15	9 am	Bay duties, looset and preparation for move. Voluntary Church Parade held.	
		2-4 p	No 1. Section practised transport work on training Ground march D.M.G.O.	
	16	8.15 am	Company move off with full Transport to march to STEENBECQUE Area	
HOULERON		12.30 pm	Company arrives in STEENBECQUE Area. Several men fell out on the march with foot trouble, mostly	
			men attached from Infantry. Two men to Hospital.	
	17	4.45 am	Company move off with full Transport to march with Brigade to the CAESTRE area.	
L'EGERREEST		9.30 am	Arrival in CAESTRE area. Company accomodated in tents. No casualties on march. Two men granted leave	
	18	8 am	Company move off with full Transport to march with Brigade to the EECKE area.	
LE GARREUX		10 am	Arrival in EECKE area. No casualties on march. Company accomodated in billets.	
	19	4.15 am	Company moves off with full Transport to march with Brigade to PROVEN (P.5) area.	O.T.W.

T2134. Wt. W708—776. 500000. 4/15. Sir J. C. & S.

Army Form C. 2118.

F. 125.

WAR DIARY
or
INTELLIGENCE SUMMARY.
(Erase heading not required.)

Instructions regarding War Diaries and Intelligence Summaries are contained in F. S. Regs., Part II. and the Staff Manual respectively. Title pages will be prepared in manuscript.

Place	Date	Hour	Summary of Events and Information	Remarks and references to Appendices
E. PROVEN.	1917 July 19 (cont.)	9 a.m.	Arrival in PROVEN (P.5.) Area. Company accommodated in tents.	
		11 a.m.	Major Arthur Richard Pipon Joseph Mary Viscount Southwell took over command of the company from Major F.A.F. Bone who went to the Machine Gun Corps Base Depot.	
		5 p.m.	The acting G.O.C. Bde. Lt.Col. F.W. Smith D.S.O. held an officers' conference.	
		3 p.m.	C.O. held officers' conference re forthcoming operations.	
	20.	10 a.m.	C.O.'s inspection of the Company in fighting order, also the Transport. Three men evacuated. Unfit. Attached men returned to duty with their units, and exchange made.	
		2 p.m.	Conference of O.s.C. units held by actg. G.O.C. Bde. Lt.Col. Hayes, D.S.O. Brig. General Gynn-Thomas D.S.O. took over command of the Brigade.	
	21	7.25 a.m.	Company moved off with full Transport to march with Brigade to the Corps Staging Area.	
ST. SIXTE.		9 a.m.	Arrival of Company in Corps Staging Area: accommodated in bivouacs in a wood.	
			One man arrived from leave. One man granted leave to U.K.	
	22	10.30 a.m.	Church of England parade service held, followed by celebration of Holy Communion.	
		10 a.m.	Nonconformist service held. Roman Catholic service also held in ST. SIXTE Church.	
			Lieut. Yeardley, O.C. Barrage Section, carried out reconnaissance in W. lines with the D.M.G.O. Anti. Southern and 5 other ranks forwarded to No.9 Squadron R.F.C. for 3 days A.A. observation course.	JHA

Army Form C. 2118.

F. 126.

WAR DIARY
or
INTELLIGENCE SUMMARY.
(Erase heading not required.)

Instructions regarding War Diaries and Intelligence Summaries are contained in F.S. Regs., Part II. and the Staff Manual respectively. Title pages will be prepared in manuscript.

Place	Date	Hour	Summary of Events and Information	Remarks and references to Appendices
ST. SIXTE	1917 July 23.	10 am	Rehearsing loading & movement of tanks with Gun Teams for forthcoming operations. See Field L.F. Bargun granted leave to United Kingdom 24.7.17. to 3.8.17. also 2 O.R.'s.	
"	24.	9.30 am	Completion of section in Battle Kit.	
		2-12 pm	Rehearsal of carrying profiles and Gun teams, for movement and action in the attack. One O.R. evacuated to Base. One reinforcement arrived.	
"	25.	9 am	Testing of Guns. Trench digging fatigues in camp.	
		to 12 noon	C.O. & 2nd in command made reconnaissance of tracks to & from the line. Lieuts. Southon and 5 O.R.'s returned from A.A. Observation Course with 9th Squadron R.F.C. Lieut. Southon and 12 O.R.'s proceeded to the 38th Div. Reinforcement Camp HERZEELE.	
"	26	9 am to 12 noon	Rehearsal of Gun team tactical movements in the attack, and how to obtain cover from view.	
		12 noon 2-4 pm	Cleaning of Gun kit, Guns, Clothing and arms. One sergeant evacuated G.C.C.S.	
"	27	7 am	Company moves off to relieve the 114th. Machine Gun Company in the ZWAANHOF SECTOR	
		2.30 pm	Barrage Section arrived & to be in action by 5 pm.	
		5 pm	Relief complete, with all four Sections and 15 guns in the line.	
YPRES SALIENT			Continuous bombardment by our artillery continuing. Enemy retaliated at intervals with 5.9" Howitzer Fire. One O.R. killed, one wounded, and one evacuated to C.C.S. (N.Y.D.)	GW

T2134. Wt. W708—776. 500000. 4/15. Sir J. C. & S.

Army Form C. 2118.

F.124.

WAR DIARY
or
INTELLIGENCE SUMMARY.
(Erase heading not required.)

Place	Date	Hour	Summary of Events and Information	Remarks and references to Appendices
YPRES SALIENT	1917 July 28	1 am. 6.3 am.	Enemy shells Coy. H.Q. with 500 shells. Our bombardment continued day and night. Enemy retaliates mostly with 500 shells on the Reutre lines and a small amount of counter battery work with heavy howitzers. Two O.R. wounded, one man gassed. Enemy expected to make a counter attack on our positions captured by the Division on our left. Wired two machine guns in the position fortified for	
		9 p.m. - 10 p.m.	Enemy commences bombing our front line. Our bombardment increased to great intensity, and continued during the night. Tanks were moved up over Canal. During day we had four wounded O.R. (two of whom were gassed.) Two O.R.'s from Reserve Spent a good deal of the day firing up Points of Assembly for "Z" day. Our Bombardment continued, enemy retaliation not so marked.	
"	29 ("X" DAY)		C.O. holds an Officers' conference. 3 O.R.'s wounded.	
"	30 ("Y" DAY)	8 a.m.	Operation orders issued. 60 mens' rations "gassed" during the night and much coys' property destroyed. Also 1 days' water supply destroyed owing to petrol tin containers being hit by shrapnel. Company is ordered to proceed to Brigade H.Q. Second-in-command	
		8 p.m.	Zero minus two hours. Company Headquarters dissolves - C.O. and 2 signallers proceed to Brigade H.Q. Second-in-command	C.T.H.

Army Form C. 2118.

F. 128.

WAR DIARY
or
INTELLIGENCE SUMMARY.
(Erase heading not required.)

Place	Date	Hour	Summary of Events and Information	Remarks and references to Appendices
YPRES SALIENT	1917 July 30	8.30. p.m.	1 and cooks, orderly room, and H.Q. forces to Transport lines at COPPERNOLLEHOEK. Gun teams in line reinforced to battle strength.	
	31 ("Z" DAY)	3.50 a.m.	Zero hour. In conjunction with several other Divisions, the 38th Div. attacked the German lines. Bombard. and reached record intensity. The 115th Brigade was in Divisional Reserve. No.1 Section took part under Lieut. Yeatby and Lieut. Miller, in the Corps Machine Gun Barrage, and fired from 3.53 to 5.7 a.m. No.3 Section had one Sect section attached to 11th. S.W.B. under Sgt Duncan and one Subsection to 14th. R.W.F. under Lieut. Gedding, Nos 2 & 4 Sections were behind these two Battns; all three Sections in assembly positions.	
		5.20 a.m.	Company H.Qrs forward in above order.	
		6 a.m.	PILCKEM RIDGE captured.	
		7.30 a.m.	First Pack mule convoy under Lieut Brown assisted by the C.S.M. moved forward from near ELVERDINGHE with bell Luccas, S.A.A., tools, sandbags, and water. They sustained in the journey three attack, one driver killed, one horse & one mule killed, two mules wounded. Reached IRON CROSS RIDGE DUMP.	
		9 a.m.	Brigade captures a line 200ˣ yards N.W. of the River STEENBEEK with battle outposts	OTH

Army Form C. 2118.

F. 129.

WAR DIARY
or
INTELLIGENCE SUMMARY.
(Erase heading not required.)

Instructions regarding War Diaries and Intelligence Summaries are contained in F. S. Regs., Part II. and the Staff Manual respectively. Title pages will be prepared in manuscript.

Place	Date	Hour	Summary of Events and Information	Remarks and references to Appendices
YPRES SALIENT	1917 JULY 31.		helped to on the East side. Lieut. Gregory with No.3 Section consolidated this line	
		4 p.m.	Enemy counter attacked from LANGEMARCK. Our S.O.S. Barrage opened to full intensity and drove off the counter attack. Nos.1,2 + 4 Sections under Lieut. Stailor Lieut.s SWINNY and THOMPSON + Miller helped to form a Machine Gun Barrage from the Eastern slopes of IRON CROSS RIDGE, on to the western exits of LANGEMARCK.	
		about 9 p.m.	Enemy again counter attacked, and was again driven off after two hours intense bombardment. 150-0 prisoners passed through the XIV Corps during the day. Our casualties as yet unknown Lieut. Yeatley was wounded about 4 p.m.	

O.T. Hale.
Lieut. 115 Machine Gun Co.

Army Form C. 2118.

WAR DIARY
or
INTELLIGENCE SUMMARY.
(Erase heading not required.)

WAR DIARY.

115 Machine Gun Company.

August 1917.

Place	Date	Hour	Summary of Events and Information	Remarks and references to Appendices

WAR DIARY
or
INTELLIGENCE SUMMARY.
(Erase heading not required.)

Army Form C. 2118.

Place	Date	Hour	Summary of Events and Information	Remarks and references to Appendices
YPRES SALIENT	1917 August 1		Company Headquarters established on IRON CROSS RIDGE. Since yesterday enemy busy spotting with aeroplanes over our positions, also in sniping. Coy. rations lost not delivered. Innojoett.	
		3 p.m.	After a bombardment mainly with 5.9" of our front and support line the enemy launched a counter attack from LANGEMARCK (trying to our "S.O.S." Artillery Barrage being a little late in commencing, machine guns were largely instrumental in rendering this attack what it resulted in, namely, a complete failure. The enemy did not reach our front line, but afterwards this was withdrawn from the valley of the STEENBEEK 200ˣ back on to higher ground. Outposts were left in the STEENBEEK. In this attack we had 12 guns firing, 8 forming Corps Barrage in conjunction with the 196th and 217th M.G.Coys. and 4 firing direct from the front line. (No.3 Section under Lieut. Godding). This Section suffered very heavily, losing 3 guns and kit, and having 6 killed & 20 wounded.	
	2	9 a.m.	The company was relieved by the 113th M.G.Co. with the exception of No.2 Section which remained in defence of the "Blockline" with guns at HOUSE 10 and ZOUAVE HOUSE. Headquarters established on CANAL BANK about C.13.c.10.9. (Sheet 28 N.W.) On arrival here orders were received to relieve the 214th M.G.Co. After rations had been issued	
		7.30 a.m.	and thermos crates for two or three hours, the company moved off to the relief.	GTY

T2134. Wt. W708—776. 500000. 4/15. Sir J. C. & S.

WAR DIARY or INTELLIGENCE SUMMARY

Army Form C. 2118.

Place	Date	Hour	Summary of Events and Information	Remarks and references to Appendices
YPRES SALIENT (cont.)	1917 Aug. 2	8.30 p.m.	Owing to the continuous rain and the state of the ground, pack mules were unable to carry the puns up as far as the old British Frontline, and "going" was very slow and difficult with the men carrying.	
		9.30 p.m.	Enemy prepares to counter-attack but is beaten off before reaching our lines also before S.O.S. Barrage.	
		11 pm	Company reports fourth night on the ground near BOCHE HQ. (PILCKEM.)	
	3	6.30 a.m.	Relief of 217th M.G.C. The company will have only 4 guns in action taken over the barrage positions on the reverse slopes of IRON CROSS RIDGE (between PILCKEM and LANGEMARCK.) Weather conditions still very unsatisfactory, and there being very little shelter, the men began to feel generally unfit from exposure. The retired hurricanes are coming up ready to and.	
	4	9 pm	Enemy again attempted to counter attack, but was driven off by our S.O.S. Barrage. We experienced great difficulty in getting the puns into positions. Positions 5,000. Remained in position all day, but owing to bad weather conditions no work of importance took place.	
	5	2 pm	Half an hour concentrated bombardment of LANGEMARCK. 2nd in command forwards	OTH

Army Form C. 2118.

WAR DIARY
or
INTELLIGENCE SUMMARY.
(Erase heading not required.)

Place	Date	Hour	Summary of Events and Information	Remarks and references to Appendices
YPRES SALIENT (cont)	1917 Aug 5	2.30 p.m.	To 114 Brigade H.Q. for fighting orders, the 115th Bde. having been relieved by them during the night of the 4th/5th. During the night of the 5th/6th the 60th Brigade relieved the 114th Brigade and on completion of relief the front line, the company had orders to move back.	
	6	6 a.m.	Company lines from Crazo Ridge advance	
		3.30 a.m.	Company arrived at Transport lines on CANAL BANK and loads up limbers. After cleaning up and had hot breakfast, men marched	
			to ELVERDINGHE CHATEAU where the men cleaned up and had hot breakfast.	
		10 a.m.	Company entrain at ELVERDINGHE.	
ST. SIXTE	7	11 a.m.	Arrives ST. SIXTE and proceeds to the XIV Corps Staging Area No. 2. Orders received to indent for all deficient kit and re-equip as soon as possible.	
			Total casualties sustained in recent operations are:– OFFICERS:– Wounded in action Lieut. E. Yearsley and 2 accidentally wounded Lieuts. Wm. Marles and 2nd Lieut. D. Bevan.	
			OTHER RANKS:– Killed in action 12, wounded in action 44 and missing 2. evacuated sick, 5 sick cases = M. To Hospital 6.	
		9 a.m. to 12 noon	Checking and noting of all deficiencies of limber stores, Gum kits, Spare Parts, and personal kit and equipment.	
		2.30 p.m.	Pay Parade.	874

WAR DIARY

Army Form C. 2118.

(Erase heading not required.)

Place	Date	Hour	Summary of Events and Information	Remarks and references to Appendices
ST. SIXTE.	1917 Aug. 8		Company resting prior to going up for engagement. Conscious collated & Casualty Rep. 5. – Wounded 5497 Pte. Phelps R.J. (1st-10th) 1/8/17.	
			Previously reported missing, now killed, now reported evacuated CCS 4/8/17 6/8.	
			Rolls 7. 1st. 2nd. 1/B/18/17. Previously reported missing, now reported 40283	
			Pte. Thompson 7 10 Sects 6/8/17. Now report the missing 20798 Pte. Mun. J.W.	
			Sect. 6/8/17.	
	9 & 10 Aug		Cleaning up Parades. Equipment, Gumboots	
		12 noon	Check of Spare Pot. Batty	
		2pm	Issue of Rum in regiment	List revised & D.R. returned	
				From Entrenment camp Westgate.
	10 Aug	8.30–9.15	Cleaning up Pastres	
		9.15	C.O. Inspection	
		10.30 a.m	Inspection by O.C. 118 Infantry Brigade.	
		2–4 p.m	Inspection of Kits, Quarter by Roth, Company Buildings	
		5.30–6	Lecture - Intercommunication Evacuated Rs of 10 4217–612	
			Pte. Dembat a/2/8/17. From Hospital arrived Pte. Stuckey 136 2/8/17	
			21 Reinforcements arrived from Base Depot 7/8/17	

A6945 Wt. W14422/M1160 350,000 12/16 D. D. & L. Forms/C.-2118/14.

WAR DIARY
or
INTELLIGENCE SUMMARY.
(Erase heading not required.)

Army Form C. 2118.

Instructions regarding War Diaries and Intelligence Summaries are contained in F. S. Regs., Part II. and the Staff Manual respectively. Title pages will be prepared in manuscript.

Place	Date	Hour	Summary of Events and Information	Remarks and references to Appendices
Silly	1917 Aug 11	5.15-?	Cleaning up horses. Reviewed lorry inspection Parade	
		9 AM	Inspection Parade	
		9.45-11.15	Gun drill 10.15-11.15 Stances taken 11.30-12.15 Physical drill. The following Promotions were made 2nd Cl S.S. Brown to corporal	
			No 4 Section Lieut. Am Instructional 2/S Cordwain 2nd class Middleton Transport Officer 11111 to be acting Sergt 16603 Corporal Smythe	
			to be 2 corpl. 1811 27266 Cpl Riddle Gr 6707 Palmer 26717	
			Upholsterey to acting Corporals 2720 No Gunner 1811 27572 Upholsterey Tr tobe Corlm L/Cp	
			2725 H.C. Plat in 7063 Gunner 18.11 to No 3 Column 10 S11	
			who Hoylenda cuph 62899 Plantampt. H.3 cclsob to 947	
			11809 Hutmake L/Cpl w/Schrn to 947 3yrs Pte Harvey L/Sqt & apparent Armoures	
	12	10pm	Church Parade	
	13	6.30-7.30	Reveille Training 9am C.O.'s Inspection	
		9.15-11.45	Advanced Drill 11.30-12.05 Physical Training 2-4pm Vaccination	
		5.30-6.0	Lecture to NCOs NCOs Mag Turley & War of Weapons 8-8.30pm 25th Bn	

Place	Date	Hour	Summary of Events and Information	Remarks and references to Appendices
G. Cpt.	19/7/13		a storm carried form Bandstand and Performance	
	14	6.30 pm	Recreational Service Gen. C.O. Preparation & Performance P.H. Welsh.	
		9.30–10.25	Gun Drill. 10.20–11.15. Immediate Action	
		11.30–1.15	Preparations 2–4pm. Coy's Foster Parker N.C.O's Mtg. Meeting of Musgrove	
			Previously reported wounded now reported "Died of Wounds" 26091 Gunn. Rea T/Lieut. 11/7/17	
	15	6.45am	Bathing	
		10 am	C.O's Preparation	
			Recreation Corporal Elam 10.15–11.15 pm Barrage Drill.	
			wounded 2499 Bombdr. H. Myers at H.Q's at 7	
	16	6.30–7.15	Reveille Inspection 9–12.15pm Coy Drill. Immediate Action & Physical Energy	
		2–4pm	Repair & Refreshments to Gun-pits. Range Finder Practice & Prototype Whistles	
			109 hrs evacuation to camp for practice	
			27285 Corporal Plant W. escorted the Military Medal.	
	17		Company washed to be ready to move at the close at 1 hours notice. Rocky bombs making arrangement for moving all the Guns. Lmms were for 10 guns whilst	
			e. Gaggy Rail.	
	18		The Company moved into the line. taking up position in Wood S.W. of Cheuflet for barrament	

WAR DIARY or INTELLIGENCE SUMMARY

Army Form C. 2118.

Place	Date	Hour	Summary of Events and Information	Remarks and references to Appendices
St Jul[e]	18.		Transport lines moved to B 29.a. Lieut R.A. Golding left in charge of xxx lines. 2 Lt Thompson & 7 men proceed to Reinforcement Camp at Alberge	
LANGEMARCK	23		Company in position on the West exit of Stenbach woods. Enemy artillery being active at night. S.O. Sergt King shown.	
	24th		Casualties avoided during this period being 10 men, four very slightly.	
	27th		Lieuten[an]t. xxx took up position being xxx the enemy was very active at Company HQ. During the period we have also very slightly, frequently shelling our position.	
			On the afternoon of the 27th the 16th xxx relieved the Company. Battalion was 158 xx. There objective being the Cap Louis. The first objective was gained but the attack was held up by M.G. fire from the L Enciente. The Infantry having suffered heavy loss and withdrew at dawn.	
			H Company then relieved in the night by 29th-30th in support to L2 Cheviot	
	30th		On Officer 10 men x xxx xxx to relieve him for A.S. xxx Lieut Hills & 3 Govt. proceeded Hq School Gunners Cavalry xxx The x	

WAR DIARY
or
INTELLIGENCE SUMMARY.

Army Form C. 2118.

Place	Date	Hour	Summary of Events and Information	Remarks and references to Appendices
L.Z. Evermingem	Aug 1917 30		period in the line 11th to 29th were as follows Officers - 2 Wounded (R.N. Frost) †† 1 Wounded (remand at duty) Other Ranks Killed 1, Died of Wounds 2, Wounded 4. Burst (Ministry) Eversullis (ind) 4	
"	31		Company resting & new drawing up Battery Lieut R.G. Golding moved the Milking Cross	

R.N. Frost
for. O.C. 115 M.G. Coy.

WAR DIARY
or
INTELLIGENCE SUMMARY.
(Erase heading not required.)

Army Form C. 2118.

115 Machine Gun Company

1st September to 30th September 1917

Army Form C. 2118.

WAR DIARY
or
INTELLIGENCE SUMMARY.
(Erase heading not required.)

Instructions regarding War Diaries and Intelligence Summaries are contained in F. S. Regs., Part II and the Staff Manual respectively. Title pages will be prepared in manuscript.

Place	Date	Hour	Summary of Events and Information	Remarks and references to Appendices
MAKAROFF FARM	1.9.17	10.15am	C. of E. Church Parade.	
			Major Southwell resumes acting D.M.G.O. Lt. A.C. Gosling M.C. takes command of 115 M.G. Coy.	
Do	2.9.17		2nd Lt. Paull & H.W. joined Coy from Base Depôt and 27 reinforcements.	
Do	3.9.17		Preparations for the line; guns &c.	
Do	4.9.17		Do.	
Do	5.9.17	12.00n	Three guns (for A.A. defence) at JOLIE FM. C.2.d.5.6 and C.2.a.5.0 relieved by 3 guns of 113 M.G. Coy.	
		1.0pm	16 teams of three men each, with carriers & accessories moved off to relieve 1/6 M.G. Coy in support line near AU BON GITE. Relief completed by 5.30 P.M. Coy Hq at VULCAN CROSSING.	
On the R. STEENBEEK	5.9.17 to 9.9.17		16 guns occupied a line of shell holes running S.E. from AU BON GITE for 900 yds, two men per gun, with a third in reserve in a dugout. No S.O.S. call was made during this time, two rounds were fired	

A6945 Wt. W11422/M1160 350000 12/16 D.D. & L. Forms/C./2118/14.

WAR DIARY
or
INTELLIGENCE SUMMARY.
(Erase heading not required.)

Army Form C. 2118.

Instructions regarding War Diaries and Intelligence Summaries are contained in F. S. Regs., Part II. and the Staff Manual respectively. Title pages will be prepared in manuscript.

Place	Date	Hour	Summary of Events and Information	Remarks and references to Appendices
ON RSTEEN-BEEK	5.9.17 to 9.9.17		Shelling was very heavy and casualties occurred: 5 killed, 1 died of wounds, 10 wounded (of whom 6 by gas shell) One M.G. was completely destroyed, and much equipment burned. One telephony was broken during this period.	
	10.9.17	4.30 AM	115 Coy relieved by 59 M.G. Coy, relief complete by 6.0 a.m. Coy returned to transport lines BRIDGE JUNCTION. Coy entrained at ELVERDINGHE 1.5to for P5 Area, arrived in camp at 6.10 P.M.	
P5 AREA	11.9.17	9.0-10.0 AM	Baths at COUTHOVE.	
P5 AREA	12.9.17	9.15 AM	Parade to move to ERRE AREA. Coy HQ at Q.Y.q.9.6. Men attached to 115 M.G.C. from 10th, 11th S.W.B. and 19th R.W.F. relieved to their units.	
MORBECQUE	13.9.17	10.15 AM	Move to MORBECQUE AREA. Arrived 2.10 P.M. H.Q. + billets LA HAUTE LOGE.	
ESTAIRES	14.9.17	7.30 AM	Move to ESTAIRES AREA. Arrived in camp 20Q', near canal, LA GORGUE.	

Army Form C. 2118.

WAR DIARY
or
INTELLIGENCE SUMMARY.
(Erase heading not required.)

Instructions regarding War Diaries and Intelligence Summaries are contained in F. S. Regs., Part II. and the Staff Manual respectively. Title pages will be prepared in manuscript.

Place	Date	Hour	Summary of Events and Information	Remarks and references to Appendices
LA GORGUE	15.9.17	10 am / 12:30 pm	Preparation of Sections 1, 2 & 4 for the line. Preparation for move to ARMENTIERES.	
	16.9.17	4:15 pm	Coy moved off for ARMENTIERES. Arrived at Coy Hq H6a25E3 at 10:00 a.m.	
		7:0 am	Sections 1, 2 and three relieved three sections of 170 M.G. Coy in the line. Relief complete 7.0 a.m.	
ARMENTIERES	17.9.17		Coy Hq and Section Hq taken over. 2/Lt Thompson, Hall, Paull and Schulte in the line.	
"	18.9.17		Re-adjustment of gun pits. Major Southwell returned from Div Hq at Millbrydon Farm D'15.	
"	19.9.17		Survey of gun positions.	
	20.9.17	1:0 –	Lt Gudding M.C. W Leave to U.K. Reserve section withdrawn gun fired 3000 rounds on enemy	
	21.9.17	3:40 am	relief in WEZ MACQUART 1:0 – 4:00 a.m.	
		9:30 am	"A" Section to Leave W.D.R.	
	22.9.17	4:50 am	Relief of Officers in the line, exchange of duties and re arrangement of firing of machine guns.	

WAR DIARY or INTELLIGENCE SUMMARY.

Army Form C. 2118.

(Erase heading not required.)

Place	Date	Hour	Summary of Events and Information	Remarks and references to Appendices
ARMENTIERES	22/9/17	10pm 7pm	Anti gas Raw relief completed by 7.0pm	
	23/9/17	10:30am	C of E parade 10.30 am at JUTE FACTORY.	
		9-10am	Nos 1 & 2 of reserve section reconnoitre reserve area positions & selected gun pits.	
		6.00pm	Standby orders for billet issued	
	24/9/17		Thorough reconnaissance of three posts & places to be commenced	
	25/9/17		One man wounded by shell fire in CENTRAL AVENUE (C. Trench)	
	26/9/17		Continuation of above - eventually all wire on R. sector	
	27/9/17	2.0- 5.0pm	Baths at LAUNDRY. Night firing commenced from Subsidiary Line Northeast by type 5000 rounds per night	
	29/9/17	11.00am	L/Cpl T Hale and three O.R. returned from Small Arms Course Camiers	

WAR DIARY
or
INTELLIGENCE SUMMARY.
(Erase heading not required.)

Army Form C. 2118.

Place	Date	Hour	Summary of Events and Information	Remarks and references to Appendices
ARMENTIERES	30/9	11.30 a.m.	Enemy observation balloon reported from our Sector H4 where there were 4 or 5 drifting N.W. at a height of about 300 ft over Tissages. It was floating perpendicularly end up.	
	30/9	7.30 p.m.	Count of enquiry on alarm balloon which was drawn by Artillerie observer by 2/Lt Hall. Night firing ceased till further orders. Church Parade at Jute Factory. Increased artillery activity on both sides.	

A.Y. Brown
2/Lt.
for O.C. 113 M.G.Coy.

Army Form C. 2118.

WAR DIARY
or
INTELLIGENCE SUMMARY.
(Erase heading not required.)

Vol 18

115 Machine Gun Company

War Diary

October 1917.

WAR DIARY
INTELLIGENCE SUMMARY
(Erase heading not required.)

Army Form C. 2118.

Place	Date	Hour	Summary of Events and Information	Remarks and references to Appendices
ARMENTIÈRES	1917 Oct. 1	8.30am to 11.15am 1-1.30pm	Enemy shelled front & support line rapidly with H.E. at 1/2 hourly intervals. Our artillery retaliated at intervals. Rifle and M.G. activity. Lieut. A.C. Godding (M.C.) returned from leave. Relieved with H.T.M.B. 30 shells at PRINCENTRES 10-11.30pm.	
"	2		Slight trench mortar activity beginning on outpost line. Otherwise quiet day. Only one enemy aeroplane seen.	
"	pm.		Harassing fire carried out from 9pm-12 midnight. Rounds fired 40-20.	
"	3		No enemy aerial activity. Slight artillery and T.M. activity on outpost lines at intervals. Harassing fire carried out during night 3/4. Rounds fired 2000. Our artillery only fired in retaliation. Lieut. P. Godsmark (M.M.) joined the company as Transport Officer.	
"	4	9.30am 5.0-8.0pm	H.V. shells on HOUPLINES ROAD. Enemy artillery fairly active during day on our communication trenches with 7.7 mm, 10.5 cm, & 15 cm Howitzer. Enemy aircraft fairly active. Our artillery carried out counter-retaliation and counter battery work. Hostile V.B. firing retired from line.	
"	5	4am 6, 9.30 3.15 pm 6 pm	Enemy artillery again fairly active on communication trenches and the Subsidiary line. 100 rounds fired anti-aircraft. Enemy planes flew over at 1.30 p., 2 pm, 5 pm. 30 of our planes flew over German lines. Our planes active all night 5/6th. Harassing Fire carried out during night 5/6th. Rounds fired 2000.	

C.J.Hale Lieut. Col.

WAR DIARY
INTELLIGENCE SUMMARY
(Erase heading not required.)

Army Form C. 2118.

Place	Date	Hour	Summary of Events and Information	Remarks and references to Appendices
ARMENTIÈRES	1917 OCT. 6	10 a.m.	Our artillery fired 100 rounds on enemy front line system. Enemy artillery quiet day.	
		16.12 noon		
		4-5p	CAMBRIDGE HOUSE and FUSILIER AVENUE were shelled, and two bombs during the night were targets.	
			2 Lieut. Bensley 121 ST. Brigade R.F.A. attached to the Company.	
			and 2 Lieut. V.L. Sunning proceeded to 21st Brigade R.F.A. for instruction, exportation etc.	
"	7	1 a.m.	"Winter Line" commenced. Watches put back to 12 midnight.	
		10 a.m.	12 15 cm Howitzer shells near SQUARE FARM (I.9.a.)	
		6.30 a.m.	Enemy machine gun active 470. Subsiding line and FOKER also active.	
			Aerial activity with video during the morning. 390 rounds with aircraft.	
			Lieut B.T. McLennan 280 on leave.	
"	8		Very quiet day. A little aerial activity. Enemy machine grouping over advancing line. Very rainy and windy night.	
		6.30 p.m.		
"	9		Aeroplane up with little altitude during day. Two anti-aircraft guns firing IRISH ARIZONA. Anti T.M.s artillery retaliated.	
"	10		Enemy aircraft fairly active during day, but owing to very high ammunition fires, and little, no one was carried out. 4 our anti-aircraft	
			One N.C.O. proceeded to Divisional Gas School.	

A.T. Makhur 4

Army Form C. 2118.

WAR DIARY
INTELLIGENCE SUMMARY.
(Erase heading not required.)

Instructions regarding War Diaries and Intelligence Summaries are contained in F. S. Regs., Part II. and the Staff Manual respectively. Title pages will be prepared in manuscript.

Place	Date	Hour	Summary of Events and Information	Remarks and references to Appendices
ARMENTIÈRES	1917 OCT. 11		Moderate artillery activity on both sides. Harassing fire carried out during night	
			11th/12th Rounds fired 300.0	
		5.30 p.m.	Numerous enemy aeroplanes overhead. Moderately shelling with no effect. Our aeroplanes most of the time. 1200 rounds anti-aircraft fired.	
			Huns aeroplanes fired 113 M.G.s	
		5.20 p.m.	Rope fire ? Kies Wind enemy line.	
	12	12.45 a.m.	Heavy gas shell bombardment in the direction of NIEPPE. Fire reported	
		6.1.15 a.m.	yesterday was running brightly at Ans Farm till 2 a.m.	
			Intermittent artillery activity on both sides. 4 enemy aeroplanes	
			attacked our aeroplane observing machines but something rather	
			shells. No rounds anti-aircraft fired.	
			Harassing fire carried out during night 12th/13th Rounds fired 300.0	
	13	11.30 a.m.	Enemy fifteen planes over Sailly flew over subsidiary line. Batteries after A.A. shelling began. 1000 rounds harassing fire during night 13th/14th was fired.	
			Hr. F. Schiela attacked to 121st Bde. "B" Batty. R.F.A. for instruction. Co-operation to ? witch Wilson	
			arrived here R.F.A. for same purpose	

A6945 Wt. W14422/M1160 350,000 12/16 D.D. & L. Forms/C./2118/14.

Army Form C. 2118.

WAR DIARY
INTELLIGENCE SUMMARY.
(Erase heading not required.)

Instructions regarding War Diaries and Intelligence Summaries are contained in F. S. Regs., Part II, and the Staff Manual respectively. Title pages will be prepared in manuscript.

Place	Date	Hour	Summary of Events and Information	Remarks and references to Appendices
ARMENTIÈRES	1917 Oct. 14		Enemy Aircraft fairly active — 1650 rounds anti-aircraft fired. A few enemy shells on ARMENTIÈRES.	
		6.30 p	Five minutes 2.4/2 fire with 21cm. Howitzers on NIEUWE HOUPLINES	
			3000 H.E. Gas & shrapnel fire during night 14th/15th on enemy dumps.	
			Two M.G.'s left for Course of M.G. School of Army.	
	15		Enemy Heavy Artillery (chiefly 21cm Hows.) active all day on communicating works and back areas.	
			Our artillery engaged in wire cutting and retaliations. 4550 rounds fired a Zwischenziele	
		10pm to 11 pm	Gas Shells on ARMENTIÈRES. 1010 rounds harassing fire on enemy communications during night	
	16		Our artillery intermittently shelled enemy Batteries and Back areas during the day.	
		11 pm	3500 rds. harassing fire during night 16/17th. 50 rounds Gas Shells on enemy.	
	17	11 pm to 6 am	Enemy tried on two different occasions Raid Activity, but to no avail. Both attempts frustrated. Both 2nd & 4th fine. anti-aircraft shelled FRÉLINGHIEN Bombing activity in flashing No. 4 Infy. Post (Front line)	
			Enemy Artillery more active than usual, especially when retaliating to our Heavy T.M.	
			Suspected Battery positions shelled at 9am, 11am, and 2pm.	
	18	5.30 pm	50 rounds 15cm How. on HOUPLINES ROAD. Our aircraft active all day and encountered	
			Interceptions relief in Nelson Rede place. Suspect Flights provided C.O. H.S. of No. 88. M.G.C.	
			Enemy Artillery busy with counter-batting shots all day, otherwise quiet day. Harassing fire during night.	C.J.H.a.

A6945 Wt. W14422/Mr160 350,000 12/16 D. D. & L. Forms/C/2118/14

Army Form C. 2118.

WAR DIARY
or
INTELLIGENCE SUMMARY.
(Erase heading not required.)

Instructions regarding War Diaries and Intelligence Summaries are contained in F.S. Regs., Part II. and the Staff Manual respectively. Title pages will be prepared in manuscript.

Place	Date	Hour	Summary of Events and Information	Remarks and references to Appendices
ARMENTIERES	1914 OCT. 19	10a.m	Major A.R.P.J.M. Viscount Southwell relinquished command of the company on proceeding to Machine Gun Corps Base Depot.	
			Captain F.C.W. Taylor took over command of the company.	
		3 p.m.	Lieut. G.T. Hale returned from leave United Kingdom.	
			Enemy artillery unusually quiet all day. Aerial activity normal. 1000 rds. fired anti-aircraft. Our artillery were quiet during morning. Later in the afternoon heavies engaged enemy front line. Harassing fire during night 19th/20th. Rounds fired 2870.	
"	20	4 a.m.	Gas shells near Schirfiery line, also Trenchmortars. Enemy Artillery fairly active all day with aeroplane doing "Spotting" work. 400 rounds fired anti-aircraft.	
		10 a.m	HW.PLANES shelled with 21 cwm. Hows. till 1 p.m.	
			1500 rounds fired during night 20th/21st. harassing enemy communications.	
"	21	10a.m to 11.30	ARMENTIERES shelled. Aerial activity normal. 1800 rds. fired anti-aircraft. 3000 rounds fired during night 21/22 on enemy C.T.'s. Enemy M.G.'s active all night.	
			Lieut. R.C. Thompson proceeded on leave to U.K. 21 - 31/10/1917. Lieut. P. Hall attached to 121st.	
"	20		Bde. R.F.A. "C" Battery for instruction, cooperation &c., Lieut. Scholes returned from "B" Battery.	
"	21		Two N.C.O's returned from A.Aircraft course.	

C.T.W. Hale

Army Form C. 2118.

WAR DIARY
INTELLIGENCE SUMMARY.
(Erase heading not required.)

Instructions regarding War Diaries and Intelligence Summaries are contained in F. S. Regs., Part II. and the Staff Manual respectively. Title pages will be prepared in manuscript.

Place	Date	Hour	Summary of Events and Information	Remarks and references to Appendices
ARMENTIÈRES	1917 Oct. 22		Very quiet day owing to bad weather. No aerial activity. Slight T.M. action by us. 300 Bs. harassing fire carried out according to programme during night 22nd/23rd.	
"	23		Activity again below normal. No aerial activity. Usual harassing fire programme carried out. 300 B.	
"	24	8 a.m.	C.O. carried out reconnaissance of the line with Mr Brigadier on HOUPLINES. Heavily shelled with 15 cm. Minifies for ¾ hour until 11 a.m.	
		12 noon to 1 pm	ARMENTIÈRES shelled. Our artillery retaliated on enemy back areas. 250 rounds fired anti-aircraft, and 7500 harassing fire during night 24th/25th.	
"	25		Enemy aircraft fairly active during the day. 250 rounds fired anti-aircraft. 10000 rounds harassing fires during night. Both artilleries quiet most of the day.	
"	26	8 a.m.	Artillery active on enemy support line. Water carried out a small trench mortar shoot covered by Field practising on enemy support line. No aerial activity. 800 rounds harassing fires during the night.	
"	27		Enemy heavy batteries active all day, morning on CHAPELLE D'ARMENTIÈRES, afternoon on ARMENTIÈRES and evening on HOUPLINES. Our heavy artillery active all day on enemy back areas. Trench mortars active on both sides. Aeroplanes busy on our	E.T. Male.

WAR DIARY

Army Form C. 2118.

(Erase heading not required.)

Place	Date	Hour	Summary of Events and Information	Remarks and references to Appendices
ARMENTIERES	1917 Oct. 27.		Contrained "spotting" for Artillery and patrolling the lines in groups. Enemy planes flew very high to avoid AA shell and m.g. fire. 1050 rds fired. 1250 rounds harassing fire during night on enemy wire.	
"	28.	12.30 p.m.	Inter section Relief begun. Finished at 8 p.m.	
			Sergeant H.C. Hardy proceeded to Officers' Cadet School — England. 2Lieut. Earl Olsson, United States Infantry, attached for instruction.	
		2 p.m.	Our left supporting subjected to an enemy T.M. bombardment. Our artillery retaliation was forceful and effective in stopping enemy fire. Aerial activity below normal owing to bad visibility all day.	
		9.30 p.m.	We fired gas projectors onto enemy lines. 15 minute continuous and intense fire. This operation was supported by heavy artillery, trench mortar and machine gun barrages for 59 minutes. Divl. M.G. Co. utilized 10 guns in this barrage, and this unit associated with 3 guns firing on enemy communication trenches. From reports received subsequently enemy did not have heavy casualties from the gas. No retaliation on the 28th inst. Rounds fired 1500 and 1500 on enemy wire after gas mortar bombardment had ceased.	

C.F. Hale

Army Form C. 2118.

WAR DIARY
~~INTELLIGENCE~~ SUMMARY.
(Erase heading not required.)

Instructions regarding War Diaries and Intelligence Summaries are contained in F. S. Regs., Part II. and the Staff Manual respectively. Title pages will be prepared in manuscript.

Place	Date	Hour	Summary of Events and Information	Remarks and references to Appendices
ARMENTIÈRES	1917 Oct. 29.	8 a.m. to 12 noon.	Active enemy retaliation, chiefly with 10 c.m. How., on the subsidiary line near Right Batten. H.Q. 30 o.r. shells here, and on CHAPELLE D'ARMENTIÈRES, LILLE Ry., cross country tracks, and CROSS CUT.	
		9 p.m.	Enemy fired wind with smoke-shells. 3 fires. No subsequent action. Aerial activity negligible. 150 o.r. fires intervening wire (gaps) during night.	
	30.		Very quiet day. 3000 o.r. harassing fire during night.	
		1 p.m.	Enemy counter battery work with 10 c.m. guns on HOUPLINES Batty. positions. Aircraft, only one enemy plane which was flying very high, seen during day.	
	31	3 p.m. & 5.30 p.m.	HOUPLINES and the right of the subsidiary line heavily shelled with heavy howitzers. Aircraft active "spotting". 200 r.r. fires anti-aircraft.	
			3000 r.r. harassing fire during the night.	
			Captain G. J. Norris M.G.C. attended for instruction.	

C.T. Halkirk.
115 Machine Gun Co.

Army Form C. 2118.

WAR DIARY
or
INTELLIGENCE SUMMARY.
(Erase heading not required.)

115 MACHINE GUN COMPANY.

WAR DIARY.

NOVEMBER 1917.

Army Form C. 2118.

WAR DIARY
INTELLIGENCE SUMMARY
(Erase heading not required.)

Instructions regarding War Diaries and Intelligence Summaries are contained in F.S. Regs., Part II. and the Staff Manual respectively. Title pages will be prepared in manuscript.

Place	Date	Hour	Summary of Events and Information	Remarks and references to Appendices
ARMENTIÈRES	1917 Nov. 1		Enemy Howitzers active all day on batteries etc. in HOUPLINES and NOUVEL HOUPLINES. Our planes active during the morning, and several heard during the night. Enemy planes busy "spotting". We fired 3000 rounds harassing fire during night 31/1st and 5500 rounds on wire work etc. during night 1st/2nd. Inter Section Relief carried out.	
"	2		Enemy Artillery activity again above normal. HOUPLINES and ARMENTIÈRES heavily shelled with 15 cm How. and Gas Shells, at times intensely, at 10.30 p.m. 1st, 4 a.m. and 5.30 a.m. 2nd. Aerial activity also above normal. Harassing fire on enemy trenches during night 2nd/3rd.	
"	3		Little activity during the day. Our artillery continued wire cutting operations. 2/Lieut. R.L. Thompson returned from leave. 8000 rounds harassing fire night 2nd/3rd.	
"	Sun.4	11 am	Church of England Parade Service held in the JUTE FACTORY—ARMENTIÈRES. Except for intermittent gas shelling over the whole Sector during night 4/5, enemy	
		10.30 pm	artillery was quieter than usual. Enemy machine guns active till 2.30 a.m. 5th.	
"	5	12.30 p.m.	Considerable volume of harassing fire by Lewis and Machine Guns was directed on the enemy wire and communications during the night. As a result of gas shelling 9 men were gassed, 2 of whom remained at duty. Inter Section Relief carried out – complete by 8 p.m. Enemy artillery and machine guns	C.T.Hak.

T2134. Wt. W708—776. 500000. 4/15. Sir J. C. & S.

Army Form C. 2118.

WAR DIARY
INTELLIGENCE SUMMARY
(Erase heading not required.)

Instructions regarding War Diaries and Intelligence Summaries are contained in F. S. Regs., Part II. and the Staff Manual respectively. Title pages will be prepared in manuscript.

Place	Date	Hour	Summary of Events and Information	Remarks and references to Appendices
ARMENTIÈRES	1917 Nov. 5.		Again quiet during the night and day. Aerial activity confined to one enemy plane and slight activity by our planes. Stokes Mortars active in conjunction with H.T.M. Bombardment of enemy front line. Harassing fire with Machine Guns continues during the night. 2 kinds. H.A.B. Miller proceeded to United Kingdom under instructions to report to War Office, and was struck off the strength accordingly.	
"	6.		We continued m.g. harassing fire during night. Our artillery continued wire cutting, and engaged back area targets. Enemy activity normal. Slightly increased aerial activity on both sides. M. Gun harassing fire continued.	
"	7.		Our's and the enemy's artillery moderately active during the day. H and L.T.M. active against enemy front line system.	
"	8.	1·24 am.	Ten Officers and 270 other ranks of the 10th Battn. South Wales Borderers successfully raided the enemy trenches near the ARMENTIÈRES – LILLE RAILWAY. At Zero our Artillery opened on enemy front line, then to support line, and afterwards in conjunction with machine guns and Stokes Mortars formed an effective "Box Barrage" for the raiders. Enemy wire was thoroughly cut and the raiding party	O.J.Wale

T2134. Wt. W708—776. 500000. 4/16. Sir J. C. & S.

Army Form C. 2118.

WAR DIARY

INTELLIGENCE SUMMARY

(Erase heading not required.)

Instructions regarding War Diaries and Intelligence Summaries are contained in F. S. Regs., Part II. and the Staff Manual respectively. Title pages will be prepared in manuscript.

Place	Date	Hour	Summary of Events and Information	Remarks and references to Appendices
ARMENTIÈRES	1914 Nov 8.		had no difficulty in entering the enemy's trenches. Two dug outs were blown up by the Royal Engineers and 14 prisoners were taken. It is estimated that at least 50 of the enemy were killed. Enemy artillery retaliation was late and never became strong. It ceased when our artillery stopped firing. A copy of the Machine Gun Scheme of this Unit is appended hereto.	
"	9	12.30 p.m.	Into action. Relief took place. Complete by 7.30 p.m. The following is a copy of a Special Coy. Order No. 1424 of 8-11-17:- "The following is a copy of a telegram received from Divisional H.Q. and addressed to Brigade H.Q.:- 'The Corps Commander congratulates all troops who took part in yesterday's raid viz The Divisional Commander directs that this message in which he most heartily concurs be communicated to all ranks.'" 62 other ranks in 14 Company granted Proficiency Pay - 56 Class I and 6 Class II. Enemy Artillery and Arial Activity increased. Gas shells again used. Night firing continued.	
"	10		Enemy Artillery unusually quiet. No aerial activity. Usual m.g. fire by us during night 10/11.	

C.J.Hall

SECRET.

To O.M.G.O. 38th Division.

Ref. Para. 10, App. III, 115th Inf. Brigade Raid Scheme.

Gun	Position	Target	Direction	Elevation	Rounds fired	Time	Remarks
C 28/1	Z	I 5d 3500	130½° G.	2° 50'	4000		
I 9/3	Y	I 11d 17.92	122½° G.	3° 10'	5000	1-24 a.m to 3-9 a.m	One firing pin broken
I 9/2		I 11d 51.85 I 11c 65.94	92½° G.	2° 30'	4.500		
Res. 1.		I 9d 52.88 I 11c 80.95	92½° G.	2° 46'	4.500	8:11:17	One fuzee spring broken
„ 2.		I 9d 53.90 I 11c 92.83	92° G.	2° 59'	4.500		
„ 3.		I 9d 56.93 I 11c 78.87	91½° G.	2° 36'	4.500		Roller became detached
„ 4.		I 9d 56.96 I 11c 64.89	91½° G.	2° 25'	4.500		

8.11.17.

J.W.Taylor Capt.
O.C. 115 M.G.Coy

Army Form C. 2118.

WAR DIARY

~~INTELLIGENCE SUMMARY~~

(Erase heading not required.)

Instructions regarding War Diaries and Intelligence Summaries are contained in F. S. Regs., Part II and the Staff Manual respectively. Title pages will be prepared in manuscript.

Place	Date	Hour	Summary of Events and Information	Remarks and references to Appendices
ARMENTIERES	1914 Nov. 11	11 a.m.	Church of England parade service in the JUTE FACTORY - ARMENTIERES. Very little activity. Enemy's fire during the day. Our trench mortars were active, covered by Artillery Fire. We directed M.S. harassing fire during the night onto an enemy railway junction and two main communication Trenches.	
"	12		No event of importance occurred during the day. Usual M.S. harassing fire directed during the night on enemy approach tracks and communications. 2 Lieut. L. F. Brown proceeded on 14 days leave to United Kingdom.	
"	13	12.30 p.m.	Inter section relief carried out and completed by 10 p.m. Enemy very active installers points with gas shells during the night. During the week 7th - 14th he has shown great activity in this direction. This Brigade front having received a record number of gas shells. This unit had a whole team of 5 men casualties, gassed and 7 men altogether have been sent home owing to the after effects which normally come on 12 to 18 hours after the attack. Points upon which the enemy directs his fire were - Field Batteries in ARMENTIERES and neighbourhood, junctions of Communication Trenches with the Subsidiary Lines, and communication trenches behind the subsidiary line. In the most forward area, gas mortars were used with effect on the support lines.	C.T. Hole

T2134. Wt. W708—776. 500000. 4/15. Sir J. C. & S.

Army Form C. 2118.

WAR DIARY
or
INTELLIGENCE SUMMARY.
(Erase heading not required.)

Instructions regarding War Diaries and Intelligence Summaries are contained in F. S. Regs., Part II. and the Staff Manual respectively. Title pages will be prepared in manuscript.

Place	Date	Hour	Summary of Events and Information	Remarks and references to Appendices
ARMENTIÈRES	1917 Nov. 14.		Enemy Artillery activity below normal. Aerial patrolling activity during the afternoon. We directed 9000 rds. m.g. harassing fire on to an enemy farm and tramways. Apparent fire from nuisance of 2 Belts & Breo additional Parvasive gun.	
"	15.		Enemy activity increased slightly by some counter-battery work in HOUPLINES and patrolling on ARMENTIÈRES. Naval harassing fire (9000 rds.) on enemy communication trenches and dumps. Normal aerial activity.	
"	16.		Little activity on either side. 9500 rds. m.g. harassing fire during night.	
"	17.	12.30 p.m.	Into Sector relief carried out. Complete by 11 p.m. Our Artillery shelled enemy dug outs and strong points. Enemy retaliated by shelling at night our communication trenches and ARMENTIÈRES.	Selector
"	18.		Marked increase in enemy artillery and aerial activity. Shelling took place all day on Battery positions and nearly all trenches in the forward area. Several hundred shells fired. M.G. Harassing fire (9000 rds.) during the night on enemy farms and a communication trench.	
"	19.		Enemy again showed marked activity, plane activity co-operating with counter-battery shoots and Huns temporarily preventing retaliation. From 10.25am to 11.15am a	

C.J. Hale

Army Form C. 2118.

Instructions regarding War Diaries and Intelligence
Summaries are contained in F. S. Regs., Part II.
and the Staff Manual respectively. Title pages
will be prepared in manuscript.

WAR DIARY
or
INTELLIGENCE SUMMARY.
(Erase heading not required.)

Place	Date	Hour	Summary of Events and Information	Remarks and references to Appendices
ARMENTIÈRES	1914 Nov. 19.	11.25 a.m.	barrage off guns of all calibres, and T.M's & M.G's was put down by the enemy behind our support and subsidiary lines in the HOUPLINES SUB-SECTOR.	
"	20.		Our 6" T.M.'s were active, and 4000 rifs m.g. harassing fire was directed on to enemy tramways and communications. Aeroplanes were also actively engaged. The Brigade sector again received much attention from enemy artillery. Battery positions and dumps received 15 cm and 10 cm. H.E. and gas during the day, and both support and subsidiary lines were shelled all day, with 7.7 cm. and 10 cm. By night enemy directed harassing fire on to his day targets. Our artillery retaliates moderately. 8000 rd.s m.g. fire during night on C.T's	
"	21.	12.30. p.m.	Inter section relief carried out. Complete at 11 p.m. 4 reinforcements arrived from 114th M.G. Coy. Enemy artillery activity was again above normal, ARMENTIÈRES and the Support line in HOUPLINES Subsects receiving most attention. Our artillery was more active in effective retaliation. Usual m.g. harassing fire.	
"	22.		Activity on both sides lessened. German patrol snipers and one dead officer (Houplier). Usual m.g. harassing fire during night 22/23. Enemy appeared nervous during the night and bombed his own wire.	C.J.Mchel.

T2134. Wt. W708—776. 500000. 4/16. Sir J. C. & S.

Army Form C. 2118.

WAR DIARY
or
INTELLIGENCE SUMMARY.
(Erase heading not required.)

Place	Date	Hour	Summary of Events and Information	Remarks and references to Appendices
ARMENTIÈRES	1914 Nov. 23.		5 Reinforcements arrived from M.G.C. Base Depot.	
"	24	4.55 a.m.	Heavy bombardment by enemy. "S.O.S." signal sent up after which our Artillery promptly opened fire. It was thought that an enemy fighting patrol was out, but an officers patrol sent out by us after the bombardment did not find anything nearer the Bombardment slackened.	
		6 a.m.		
		6.30 a.m.	Bombardment ceased.	
"	23		Enemy Artillery active all day on back areas. Gas Shells on ARMENTIÈRES during the night. Usual m.g. harassing fire.	
"	24		But otherwise much quieter after early morning attack. Usual m.g. harassing fire during the night. 10,000 rounds fired.	
"	25	12.30 p.m.	Inter section relief carried out. Completed at 9.30 p.m. Our Artillery carried out a successful destructive shoot on an enemy C.T. and neighbourhood was fired on at night by our m.g.'s (8000 rds.) Otherwise both sides were quiet.	
"	26.		The bridging line and ARMENTIÈRES heavily shelled during the morning. Our Artillery not very active. Usual m.g. harassing fire during night. (9000 rds.)	C.J.Hale

Army Form C. 2118.

Instructions regarding War Diaries and Intelligence Summaries are contained in F. S. Regs., Part II. and the Staff Manual respectively. Title pages will be prepared in manuscript.

WAR DIARY
~~INTELLIGENCE SUMMARY.~~

(Erase heading not required.)

Place	Date	Hour	Summary of Events and Information	Remarks and references to Appendices
ARMENTIÈRES	1917 Nov. 27.		Abnormal quietness all day on both sides. Enemy again bombed his wire during the night, and directed intense m.g. fire on it in several places.	
"	28.		6000 m.g. harassing fire unredirected during night on to enemy C.T.'s. Considerable movement during the day was observed on the PREMESQUES - RUELLE DE LA NOIX road. Enemy artillery generally more active. Usual m.g. harassing fire during the night.	
"	29	12.30 p.m.	Intn Section Relief carried out. Completed 9 p.m. Lieut. L. F. Brown returned from leave to U.K. Activity again below normal. Usual m.g. fire at night.	
"	30	10 a.m.	2 Lieut. Hall proceeded on leave to U.K. Moderate activity during day. Enemy shelled Intensiduary line in selected parts with 10 cm and 15 cm howitzers. Our T.M.'s (6" and L.T.M's) were active. Usual m.g. harassing fire during the night.	

O.P.Aldient [?]

30/11/1917.

115 Machine Gun Coy.
B.E.F.

Army Form C. 2118.

WAR DIARY
INTELLIGENCE SUMMARY.
(Erase heading not required.)

115 Machine Gun Coy

WAR DIARY.

DECEMBER 1917.

WAR DIARY or INTELLIGENCE SUMMARY

Army Form C. 2118.

Place	Date	Hour	Summary of Events and Information	Remarks and references to Appendices
ARMENTIERES	1917 DEC. 1		Enemy artillery active all day. ARMENTIERES - HOUPLINES & CHAPELLE D'ARMENTIERES shelled during the morning. Post 14.9.p. on C.22.c. CEMETERY DISTILLERY, Stationary hut, support trench shelled during the day. Six shells reported into ARMENTIERES during the night. Our fire was active especially to the early morning. Counter Battery and interdiction plans on selected targets during the day. 8 Enemy planes crossed our lines & aeroplanes in. We fired 4570 rounds harassing fires at night. F.G.C.M. of accused on 435 L/Col Castle 2nd guarded by 1st Bony Battery. 11 C.N.Y 2356 each 26.11.17. Promoted to L/Cpl 4906 Pte Miles 987 Pte Phelps.	
	2		Both artilleries quiet. Our artillery slightly active. In the evening further N.W. displays fire L.M. Bath Food. Enemy planes over our lines. One would activity flight. Wind fired N.N.W. rounds harassing fire at night. Reinforcements arrived for Bn.	
	3		Enemy artillery active 350 and 150 lb. shells into ARMENTIERES HMP. 11800 & Communication trenches. Artillery war activity active on nmp trenches. S.O.S. up. Our artillery fire at night. App. 1800 rds fires. We engaged E2 to.4p.m. 2 gas harassing fires at night. App. 1800 rds fired. Lt. Col. Deeton Shipworth M.B. C.I.M. L. was proceed on leave. D.V.M. Whence J. Hamovich to act as C.I.M. from evening Col.	

WAR DIARY or INTELLIGENCE SUMMARY

Army Form C. 2118.

(Erase heading not required.)

Place	Date	Hour	Summary of Events and Information	Remarks and references to Appendices
ARMENTIERES	Dec 4		Hostile artillery active. HOUPLINES Battery Support Pt. shelled. Trench Mortars active on our left flank. Enemy Trench Mortars active & answered by Stokes T.M. On enemy aero. 6.5 A.M. Our T.M. active. Enemy T.M. very active. We fired 4100 rnds H.A. & 350 rnds howr.	
	5		Quiet. Hostile artillery fired 6/0 rnds into ARMENTIERES & intermittent shelling on to hostile trenches. Our artillery active. Fired on PILCKEM 6.20 pm. On glass aero 8.50 am. Whizzed on S.O.S. aerial 6.20 pm. on E.60. Harassing fire at night 6000 rnds.	
	6		Hostile activity 300 rnds on ARMENTIERES. 100 rnds on Battery positions elsewhere. Our artillery active. Retaliated on T.M.s. No artillery. Harassing fire in enemy trenches. Our L'Mentier. We fired 6000 rnds at E.P.s & 4100 rnds during harassing fire. 6 E.A.s over our lines active. No hostile volume from bombardment. (Slow to 10 hrs.)	
	7		An infantry section relief carried out. Enemy activity normal. Our artillery active T.M.s active.	
	8		Enemy artillery active. Concentrated shelling of Rifle Supports. Our artillery normal.	
	9		Enemy artillery normal. Our artillery normal. Aircraft normal. We fired 7,500 rnds Harassing fire.	
	10		Enemy artillery active. Rifle fire opened on cable in the afternoon. Our artillery active.	

Army Form C. 2118.

WAR DIARY
or
INTELLIGENCE SUMMARY.
(Erase heading not required.)

Instructions regarding War Diaries and Intelligence Summaries are contained in F.S. Regs, Part II. and the Staff Manual respectively. Title pages will be prepared in manuscript.

Place	Date	Hour	Summary of Events and Information	Remarks and references to Appendices
ARMENTIERES	14/9 Oc		We gave harassing fire at night 7500 Rounds.	
	11.		Inter-section relief carried out. Enemy activity normal. Our activity normal. We gave 7500 Rounds harassing fire at night.	
	12.		Enemy artillery quiet. Our artillery quiet. We fire harassing fire at night 7500 Rounds fired.	
	13.		Enemy artillery quiet. Our artillery quiet. Harassing fire carried on at night 7500 Rounds fired by 9 M.G.	
	14.		Inter-Section Relief carried out. A very quiet day. Capt Moore left to command 145th.	
	15.		A very quiet day. Pte Bayer wounded by shell going to wire. Relieved by M.G. M.B. 7 Bn.	
	16.		Enemy artillery active. Our artillery active. We gave harassing fire 7500 Rounds. 2/Lt Hitchenson.	
	17.		A very quiet day. We gave thousand harassing fire at night 7500 Rounds expended.	
	18.		Hostile artillery action. Our artillery active. We gave usual M.G. M.B. 7. 7500 Rounds expended. 2/Lt Powell went on leave. Lt Campbell reported to reinforcement from 2nd Bn Dept.	
	19.		Company relieved by Lt 6th Australian M.G. Coy. On completion of relief moved to rest billets at ESTAIRES.	
ESTAIRES	20.		General cleaning up of cloth, equipment. Whole Pack at 3 p.m. Pte Gilbertson by P.G.C.M. on 17th Sept here without leave conduct I.A.L.	

Army Form C. 2118.

WAR DIARY
or
INTELLIGENCE SUMMARY.
(Erase heading not required.)

Instructions regarding War Diaries and Intelligence Summaries are contained in F.S. Regs., Part II. and the Staff Manual respectively. Title pages will be prepared in manuscript.

Place	Date	Hour	Summary of Events and Information	Remarks and references to Appendices
ESTAIRES	20 21		Company proceeded taking up defensive positions of New Moulin - line opening fire started 8:50 cms inward. Outpost driven proceeded off	
	22.		Company at training from 9.30 to 4 pm. clearing from trenches, packing limbers &c.	
	23.		After Reveill proceeded Laperre Bathing parade ch. of arms Church Parade in the morning	
	24.		Company on the training ground. P.T., F.G.D. T & football Nº 3 bed Bombs against Nº S2 Tame 461 & MR at 5.10 am 4-44 MMG practical at 7.45. C.O.	
	25.		Church Parade in the morning. Christmas dinners at 5.0 pm, won by Bugles fires 6.5 three O's Concert after the dinner	
	26.		Route March in the morning Kit inspection & various parades in the afternoon. 2nd & 4th C.M.R. relieved in the line.	
	27.		Company on training ground. P.T. E.G.D. & 2 hr lectures concluded. N C on Gordele proceeded Laperre	
	28.		Company on training ground. Physical drill. E.G.D. & Grenades exercises Golf & Gun Powder Together in afternoon	
	29.		Company on training ground. Physical drill Bayonet drill Lectures (16 wk T.M.L. as signed by word) Soc IV Corps	
	30.		Company training from F.G.C. m 38059 & Cythem between Section Church parade in the morning. Officers tactical schemes in	
	31.		Company gave exhibition of Bayonet drill before D.M.G.O. & Brigadier front F.G.C.M.o 11716 Pte. Papin L. charged with When refusing away I was not water taken from his superior Officer finding party sentence 96 days ft for 112 days Lyttle S.O.C. IV Corps. A.C. Coghey Lieut 4.C. 113 mounted Company	

Army Form C. 2118.

115 M.G. Coy
Vol 21

WAR DIARY
or
INTELLIGENCE SUMMARY.
(Erase heading not required.)

Instructions regarding War Diaries and Intelligence Summaries are contained in F.S. Regs., Part II. and the Staff Manual respectively. Title pages will be prepared in manuscript.

Place	Date 1917	Hour	Summary of Events and Information	Remarks and references to Appendices
ESTAIRES	Jan. 1		Company continued its training. The day spent on the Training Ground. O.T. Barrage fire? Explosions, Recognition during Blows. Fired W from 2.30-3.30 & Lectures on Barrage fires at night. Hyperbolic shoots H.O.E. & G.C.M. on 23003 the Chandler D.S. were possible. But R.S.A.G. patrol.	as per app.
	2		The Company carried out a Brigade M.G. tactical scheme during the morning. Cavalry parade in the afternoon. By the Getty attached to Brigade. Photographs taken by the Divisional Intelligence Officer. The G.O.C. 115 Inf Bde gave a lecture at night on "The Attack".	as per app.
	3		Company continued training. P.T., F.G.D., I.A. & Rockets practices. Very expensive.	as per app.
	4		" " " P.T. Barrage shoot, F.G.D., I.A. Inf. Company Drill. Many the P.T. Barrage shoot - 27 broke & yours have	as per app.
	5	9.0	Parade - full parading Order. 9.45am 12mm Cleaning Lumber.	as per app.
	6	8.40	Company moved from it. Billets at ESTAIRES to billets at NOULIEU.	as per app.
NOULIEU	7		Company marched to Transport lives in the morning and went in the morning. Company did in the afternoon.	as per app.
	8		Lectures at night on Barrage fire. Reindeer Powder in the afternoon.	as per app.
	9		Route March in the morning. Company Drill & Range work in the afternoon from the Bap.	as per app.
	10		P.T. in the morning & preparing guns for the Ranges.	as per app.
	11		Morning. Bathing Parade. Afternoon Infantry Drill & Cleaning Guns. Morning. P.T., F.G.b., & I.A. Afternoon Range Work Roulette Greek. The Secretary of UL.7 G.C.M. on 71/16 the Paper granted by Army Commander.	as per app.
	12		3 Reinforcements from 14 M.G. & 1 Set from 10 M.G.	as per app.

For. Tt. Rell

Army Form C. 2118.

WAR DIARY
or
INTELLIGENCE SUMMARY.
(Erase heading not required.)

Instructions regarding War Diaries and Intelligence Summaries are contained in F. S. Regs., Part II. and the Staff Manual respectively. Title pages will be prepared in manuscript.

Place	Date	Hour	Summary of Events and Information	Remarks and references to Appendices
ESTAIRES	13.		Company moved back to the Billets at ESTAIRES	
	14.	9.0	Route march in full marching order. 2.9pm Cleaning forms & Lectures	
	15.		Company moved to GARBECQ after on route to ENGUINEGATTE	
GARBECQ	16		Company moved to ENGUINEGATTE arriving there at 2.15p.	
ENGUINEGATTE	17		General cleaning up.	
	18.		Morning Range Work. Preparing guns for Range Work. Section Infantry Drill	
			Range Work Practices 8, 9, 10 fired. Bell pulley. Section Infantry Drill & Shot pant meant.	
	19.		Morning. Firing stoppages. Barrage drill & Section Infantry Drill.	
			Afternoon. Final of the Section Football Competition. Result No 1 Section O 116 - 1.	
			2.50 proceeded to the M.G.C. Comforts & Pension of War Fund by the company	
	20.		Subscribed to the Fund.	
			Sunday. No parades.	
	21.		Morning. Battery Parade. Afternoon Firing Stoppages. Barrage drill & 2nd & 3rd Lubrication removal from Lewis	
	22.		Morning. Section Infantry Drill.	
			Company on the Range in the morning. Practices 11, 12 & 13 of the Machine Gun Course fired. Barrage Drill	
	23.		Company on the Range. Practices 14 & 16 fired. Afternoon the company played 116 M.G. Coy at football and lost at football. result nil. 0. 114 Coy 1. 116 M.G.	

Army Form C. 2118.

WAR DIARY
or
INTELLIGENCE SUMMARY.
(Erase heading not required.)

Instructions regarding War Diaries and Intelligence Summaries are contained in F.S. Regs., Part II. and the Staff Manual respectively. Title pages will be prepared in manuscript.

Place	Date	Hour	Summary of Events and Information	Remarks and references to Appendices
~~AELEBY~~ ENGUINEGATTE	24		Route March all day. 4 Reinforcements from 176 m.g. by.	
	25		Field Practice. 1 + 2 found by the Company. Pay Parade in the afternoon. 2 reinforcements from A.H.T.D. A/Sgt Orrell + Corporal Whitham to Special Coum GRANTHAM	
	26	8.30	Bathing Parade. Afternoon Into Section Football Match	
	27		Sunday. No Parades.	
	28.		Visit by the G.O.C. 115 Inf. Bde. Special Barrage demonstration given by the Company	
	29		Morning. Competition for Divisional firing prize. 1.30 p.m. Frank Lecke Full Parade	
			Past & fired. Afternoon cleaning guns & Lectures. Evening Lecture on Aeroplane Photography	
			by Lieut Walker R.F.C.	
	30.		Company moved from ENGUINEGATTE to GARBECQUES by van	
GARBECQUES	31		Company moved from GARBECQUES to ESTAIRES by road	

31/1/18

J.C. Gosling Lieut
for O.C. 115 M.G. Coy
B.E.F.

Army Form C. 2118.

WAR DIARY
~~INTELLIGENCE SUMMARY~~
(Erase heading not required.)

115 MACHINE GUN COMPANY

WAR DIARY

FEBRUARY 1918

Instructions regarding War Diaries and Intelligence Summaries are contained in F. S. Regs., Part II. and the Staff Manual respectively. Title pages will be prepared in manuscript.

/M 22

Place	Date	Hour	Summary of Events and Information	Remarks and references to Appendices

Army Form C. 2118.

WAR DIARY
~~INTELLIGENCE~~ SUMMARY
(Erase heading not required.)

Instructions regarding War Diaries and Intelligence Summaries are contained in F. S. Regs., Part II. and the Staff Manual respectively. Title pages will be prepared in manuscript.

Place	Date	Hour	Summary of Events and Information	Remarks and references to Appendices
ESTAIRES	1.2.18	9 a.m.	Company Parade. Limber Property Inspection. Infantry Drill. Physical Training. Afternoon Spare Parts cleaning. Pay Parade.	Appendix A
	2.2.18	9.30 a.m.	Company Parade in full marching Order for short route march. Afternoon 3.30 Major Jenn Blackadder distributed War Ribbon. Lt. Walmsley & Cpl Smith received the ribbon of the D.C.M. & C.S.M. Dunn the medal ribbon of the M.M. Brigade Horse & Mule Show held. Sgt. Alcock awarded the 1st prize for the best turned out Transport Sergeant H/Col. Bryant awarded the 2nd prize for the best turned out pair of mules.	Appendix B
	3.2.18		Sunday. Platoon Church Parade in the morning. Inter Transport Section Competition in the afternoon. No 4 Section Winners.	Appendix C
	4.2.18	9.0	Company Parade. Inf. Section drill - Bayonet - P.T. - I.A. Afternoon E.G.D. Box Respirator Drill - Cpl. Inf. Drill.	Appendix D
	5.2.18	8.0	Company Parade for digging Mortar defences line at SAILLY	Appendix E
	6.2.18	8.0	Company Parade. Work as the previous day. 5.30 Lecture by H/Col'gn on the new rules for PSM	Appendix F
	7.2.18	8.0	Company Parade. Work carried on at SAILLY constantly necessitating alteration in Scheme broken ground. The CO major to leaving supplies which the Brigade is to use. G.S. Wagon written relieving Motor Lorry	Appendix G
	8.2.18	8.0	Company Parade. Work continued at SAILLY. Afternoon Pay Parade. 2 H/S army to Essars (U.K)	Appendix H
	9.2.18	8.0	Company Parade. Work continued at SAILLY. Two men classified by A.D.M.S as B1 to travail to Base. 33213 Sapper Leaf awarded the Belgian Croix de Guerre.	Appendix I
	10.2.18	9.30	Church Parade. Kit Inspection.	Appendix J
	11.2.18		Monday. Bathing Parade. Preparing Guns & kit for the line. CO reconnoitring the line.	Appendix K

Army Form C. 2118.

WAR DIARY
INTELLIGENCE SUMMARY
(Erase heading not required.)

Instructions regarding War Diaries and Intelligence Summaries are contained in F.S. Regs., Part II. and the Staff Manual respectively. Title pages will be prepared in manuscript.

Place	Date	Hour	Summary of Events and Information	Remarks and references to Appendices
ESTAIRES	12.2.18	9.30a	Company moved to the line (Wez Macquart Sector) 2, 3 & 4 Sections to the Chapelle d'Armentières Sector relieving 170 M.G. Coy. but M.Gs fired 2000 rounds harassing fire	Appendix A
FRONT LINE WEZ MACQUART SECTOR	13.2.18		Very quiet day. Slight shelling 15pr. Battery	J.A. Anning Lt
	14.2.18		Quiet day. Usual harassing fire by M.Gs (3000 rounds) but M.Gs fired 2000 rds on neighbourhood of INCISION AVE	J.A. Anning Lt
	15.2.18		Slight hostile artillery activity	J.A. Anning Lt
	16.2.18		Inter-Section Relief. Lt. T.F. DAVIES (transferred from 113 M.G.Co.) assumed duties as 2nd i/c of Company. Hostile artillery fired on WEZ MACQUART and CHAPELLE D'ARMENTIERES with shells of all calibres. M.Gs directed harassing fire on LARGE FARM, PETIT MORAIS, GRANDE MORAIS, and WEZ MACQUART × roads firing 4000 rounds. M.Gs also shelled CHAPELLE D'ARMENTIERES with 350 5.9s	J.A. Anning Lt
	17.2.18		Enemy artillery active all day. M.Gs fired 4000 rounds at PETIT MORAIS, WEZ MACQUART × roads harassing fire	J.A. Anning Lt
	18.2.18	9-12.30	Enemy shelled CHAPELLE D'ARMENTIERES with 250 5.9s	
			Enemy aircraft active during the day also at night	J.A. Anning Lt
	19.2.18		Lt. A.C. GOODIN G.M.C. Leave (U.K.) but M.Gs fired on PARADISE RD. WEZ MACQUART × Roads & LARGE FARM (4000 rounds)	
		1.30-7.30	Enemy shelled in the vicinity of L'ARMEE (100 rounds 4.2)	
		4-	Enemy bnt.? Bntry.? shells into CHAPELLE D'ARMENTIERES.	J.A. Anning Lt

WAR DIARY
INTELLIGENCE SUMMARY

(Erase heading not required.)

Army Form C. 2118.

Instructions regarding War Diaries and Intelligence Summaries are contained in F.S. Regs., Part II. and the Staff Manual respectively. Title pages will be prepared in manuscript.

Place	Date	Hour	Summary of Events and Information	Remarks and references to Appendices
FRANCE WEZ MACQUART SECTOR	20.2.18		Inter Section Reliefs completed 4-55 pm. Enemy planes in enemy lines, but MG.S fired on LARGE FM. Enemy artillery comparatively quiet.	M. Fenwick Lt
	21.2.18		Reserve Section moved from LAUNDRY to billets at H329.1 but MGS.	M. Fenwick Lt
		2.30	Enemy aircraft & fired a LARGE FARM of PETIT NORAIS engaged enemy aircraft CHAPELLE D'ARMENTIERES with shrapnel 3000 rounds	
		3.40		
			An enemy plane was destroyed by one of ours & fell in flames in enemy lines. During night enemy sent up numerous coloured lights, no rockets observed.	
	22.2.18	12.20am	Enemy shelled CHAPELLE D'ARMENTIERES with 5.9's & gas shells	M. Fenwick Lt
		12.50	But MGS. fired on LE QUESNE, GRAND MORAIS + WEZ MACQUART X roads 4000 rounds	
	23.2.18	4.5	Enemy put down a heavy barrage of 4.2's & 5.9's on Left Battalion front & support lines	M. Fenwick Lt
		4.30		
			Harrassing fire by out MGS during the night	
	24.2.18		Inter Section Reliefs completed 6 pm.	M. Fenwick Lt
		3-4	Enemy bombarded (5000 rounds fired)	
		4-4.55	Enemy bombarded trenches & put up Barrage lights sent up in rear of LEITH WALK to CONGREVE AVE.	
		6.30	my section went up into the line, no casualties. Wind S.W.	
		5.30	The following was intercepted from enemy	M. Fenwick Lt
			"DU HAST UNS DOCH GERUFEN" punkt ohne by out MGS (5000 rounds fired)	

WAR DIARY

INTELLIGENCE SUMMARY.
(Erase heading not required.)

Army Form C. 2118.

Instructions regarding War Diaries and Intelligence Summaries are contained in F.S. Regs., Part II. and the Staff Manual respectively. Title pages will be prepared in manuscript.

Place	Date	Hour	Summary of Events and Information	Remarks and references to Appendices
WEZ MACQUART SECTOR	25/7/18		Enemy artillery quiet. Various lights sent up by the enemy during the night. No actual bellowing. Rel. laughs against our balloons from WEZ MACQUART. But M.G.S fired and gas alarms went (fired 5000 rounds). But M.G.S. fired 5000 rounds on gap intermittent shelling by enemy were kept directed on our out trenches at change of night. Enemy aircraft active.	19 Annex. 1
	26/7/18		But M.G.S. fired 5000 rounds on gap in enemy wire. Enemy artillery shelled LA VESEE & CHAPELLE D'ARMENTIERES during the day. Enemy aircraft active.	19 Annex. 2
	27/7/18		Shrapnel on CHAPELLE D'ARMENTIERES during the day & a few shells during the night. Enemy aircraft active during the day & night. But M.G.S. fired 4000 rounds on gap in enemy wire.	19 Annex. 3
				19 Annex 4

WO 95 2562/4

36 DIVN
115 INF BRIG.
TRENCH MORTAR BTY
1916 JULY & AUG

www.ingramcontent.com/pod-product-compliance
Lightning Source LLC
Chambersburg PA
CBHW081353160426
43192CB00013B/2399